John Dawson Ross

Highland Mary

Interesting Papers on an Interesting Subject

John Dawson Ross

Highland Mary
Interesting Papers on an Interesting Subject

ISBN/EAN: 9783744712804

Printed in Europe, USA, Canada, Australia, Japan

Cover: Foto ©Thomas Meinert / pixelio.de

More available books at **www.hansebooks.com**

HIGHLAND MARY

INTERESTING PAPERS
ON AN INTERESTING SUBJECT

EDITED BY

JOHN D. ROSS

Author of "Scottish Poets in America,"
And Editor of
"Celebrated Songs of Scotland," "Round Burns' Grave,"
"Burnsiana," etc., etc.

"She died. He too is dead,
Of all her girlish graces
Perhaps one nameless lock remains ;
The rest stern time effaces.
Dust lost in dust. Not so, a bloom
Is her's which ne'er can wither ;
And in that lay which lives for aye,
The twain live on together."

ALEXANDER GARDNER

Publisher to Her Majesty the Queen

PAISLEY ; AND 26 PATERNOSTER SQUARE, LONDON

1894

Dedicated to

DUNCAN MACGREGOR CRERAR, Esq.,

Of New York,

A NATIVE OF AMULREE, BREADALBANE, PERTHSHIRE ;

A POET OF TRUE MERIT ;

AND WHO WAS THE EFFICIENT AND HIGHLY ESTEEMED SECRETARY

OF THE

NEW YORK BURNS SOCIETY,

FOR NEARLY A QUARTER OF A CENTURY.

PREFATORY NOTE.

I FEEL very confident that this little volume will be
welcomed everywhere, as the contents are both interesting and readable.

The romantic and solemn parting of the lovers on that
memorable Sabbath in May ; Mary's return from the Highlands ; her sudden death at Greenock ; the poet's anguish
on receiving the intelligence of her death, and the immortal
Lament which he afterwards gave to the world, have always
been fascinating incidents in the life of Burns to me.

While I have carefully studied the connection of the
lovers in all its details, and have eagerly read all that I
could find on both sides of the question, I have never
had reason to doubt that Mary Campbell was other
than the *warm hearted, pure, noble-minded* girl which the
poet described her to be.

The reader will here find a few of the best papers and
poems, original and otherwise, regarding Highland Mary
that have come under my notice. It is, however, quite
probable that there are even better papers and poems on the
subject (Burns's pieces of course excepted) which I have not
seen, and this being the case, gives me the opportunity of
saying in the words of worthy old Cotton Mather, "The
writer has done as well and as much as he could that whatever was worthy of a mention might have it ; and if this collection of matters be not complete, yet he supposes it may
be more complete than any one else hath made : and now he
hath done, he hath not pulled up the ladder after him :
others may go on as they please with a completer com-
posure."

JOHN D. ROSS.

126 Palmetto Street,
Brooklyn, N.Y., U.S.A.

CONTENTS.

	PAGE
THE POET'S IMMORTAL WREATH---	
Highland Lassie,	9
Will Ye Go to the Indies?	11
Highland Mary,	12
To Mary in Heaven,	14
HIGHLAND MARY, ... *Archibald Munro,*	16
CONCERNING HIGHLAND MARY, *Rev. William Wye Smith,*	25
HIGHLAND MARY, ... *Duncan Macgregor Crerar,*	45
AT THE TOMB OF HIGHLAND MARY, ... *Colin Rae Brown,*	46
BURNS AND HIGHLAND MARY, ... *Robert Reid,*	50
HIGHLAND MARY IN MARBLE, ... *George Savage,*	51
HIGHLAND MARY, ... *Rev. Arthur J. Lockhart,*	53
HIGHLAND MARY, ... *Theodore F. Woolfe, A.M., M.D.,*	58
REMINISCENCE OF HIGHLAND MARY,	68
THE MYSTERY OF MARY, ... *Peter Ross,*	72
THE COMMON WEIRD, ... *Thomas C. Latto,*	76
DR. ROBERT CHAMBERS'S VIEWS,	78
TO BURNS'S "HIGHLAND MARY," *Blackwood's Magazine,*	86
HIGHLAND MARY'S GRAVE, ... *The People's Journal,*	94
HIGHLAND MARY, ... *John H. Ingram,*	97
HIGHLAND MARY, ... *Allan Cunningham,*	101
HIGHLAND MARY, ... *Mrs. Jamieson,*	104
HIGHLAND MARY IN FACT AND FICTION, ... *Dr. William Findlay,*	108

8 *Contents.*

SONNET—HIGHLAND MARY, ...*John Macfarlane,* 113

THE MONUMENT TO HIGHLAND MARY, ... 114

PROFESSOR BLACKIE'S TRIBUTE, ... 123

BURNS'S "HIGHLAND MARY,"...*J. Cuthbert Hadden,*........ 125

THE BANKS OF AYR AND HIGHLAND MARY, ... 130

HIGHLAND MARY, ...*John Arnot,* 135

BURNS AND HIS HIGHLAND MARY, *G. Washington Moon,*..... 137

BURNS'S HIGHLAND MARY, ...*Leonard A. Morrison,*..... 139

ON SEEING A LOCK OF HIGH-
LAND MARY'S HAIR, ...*Anna M. Smith,*............. 142

HIGHLAND MARY'S GRAVE, ...*Greenock Telegraph*......... 144

HIGHLAND MARY.

THE POET'S IMMORTAL WREATH.

HIGHLAND LASSIE.

NAE gentle dames, tho' e'er sae fair,
Shall ever be my Muse's care :
Their titles a' are empty show ;
Gi'e me my Highland lassie, O.

Within the glen sae bushy, O,
Aboon the plain sae rushy, O,
I set me down wi' right good will,
To sing my Highland lassie, O,

Oh, were yon hills an' valleys mine,
Yon palace an' yon gardens fine !
The world then the love should know
I bear my Highland lassie, O,

I

But fickle fortune frowns on me,
An' I maun cross the raging sea ;
But while my crimson currents flow,
I'll love my Highland lassie, O,

Altho' thro' foreign climes I range,
I know her heart will never change,
For her bosom burns with honour's glow,
My faithful Highland lassie, O.

For her I'll dare the billow's roar,
For her I'll trace a distant shore,
That Indian wealth may lustre throw
Around my Highland lassie, O.

She has my heart, she has my hand,
By sacred truth an' honour's band !
Till the mortal stroke shall lay me low,
I'm thine, my Highland lassie, O.

Farewell the glen sae bushy, O !
Farewell the plain sae rushy, O !
To other lands I now must go,
To sing my Highland lassie, O.

WILL YE GO TO THE INDIES?

Will ye go to the Indies, my Mary,
 And leave old Scotia's shore ?
Will ye go to the Indies, my Mary,
 Across the Atlantic's roar ?

Oh sweet grow the lime and the orange,
 And the apple on the pine ;
But a' the charms o' the Indies
 Can never equal thine.

I ha'e sworn by the heavens to my Mary,
 I ha'e sworn by the heavens to be true ;
And sae may the heavens forget me,
 When I forget my vow !

Oh plight me your faith, my Mary,
 And plight me your lily-white hand ;
Oh plight me your faith my Mary,
 Before I leave Scotia's strand.

We ha'e plighted our troth, my Mary,
 In mutual affection to join,
And curst be the cause that shall part us !
 The hour and the moment o' time !

HIGHLAND MARY.

Ye banks and braes, and streams around
  The castle o' Montgomery,
Green be your woods, and fair your flowers,
  Your waters never drumlie !
There simmer first unfaulds her robes,
  An' there the langest tarry ;
For there I took the last fareweel
  O' my sweet Highland Mary.

How sweetly bloom the gay green birk,
  How rich the hawthorn's blossom,
As underneath their fragrant shade,
  I clasp'd her to my bosom !
The golden hours, on angel's wings,
  Flew o'er me and my dearie ;
For dear to me as light as life,
  Was my sweet Highland Mary.

Wi' mony a vow, and lock'd embrace,
  Our parting was fu' tender ;
And pledging aft to meet again,
  We tore oursel's asunder ;
But, Oh ! fell death's untimely frost,
  That nipt my flower sae early,
Now green's the sod, and cauld's the clay,
  That wraps my Highland Mary !

Oh pale, pale, now, those rosy lips,
  I aft ha'e kissed sae fondly !
An' closed for aye the sparkling glance
  That dwelt on me sae kindly ;
And mouldering now in silent dust
  That heart that lov'd me dearly !
But still within my bosom's core
  Shall live my Highland Mary.

TO MARY IN HEAVEN.

Thou ling'ring star, with less'ning ray,
   That lov'st to greet the early morn,
Again thou usher'st in the day
   My Mary from my soul was torn.
O Mary ! dear departed shade !
   Where is thy place of blissful rest ?
See'st thou thy lover lowly laid ?
   Hear'st thou the groans that rend his breast ?

That sacred hour can I forget ;
   Can I forget the hallowed grove,
Where by the winding Ayr we met
   To live one day of parting love ?
Eternity will not efface
   Those records dear of transports past ;
Thy image at our last embrace ;
   Ah ! little thought we 'twas our last !

Ayr, gurgling, kissed his pebbled shore,
   O'erhung with wild woods, thick'ning green,
The fragrant birch and hawthorn hoar,
   Twined amorous round the raptur'd scene ;
The flowers sprang wanton to be prest,
   The birds sang love on every spray—
Till too, too soon, the glowing west
   Proclaim'd the speed of wingéd day.

Still o'er these scenes my mem'ry wakes,
   And fondly broods with miser care ;
Time but th' impression stronger makes,
   As streams their channels deeper wear.
My Mary, dear departed shade !
   Where is thy place of blissful rest ?
See'st thou thy lover lowly laid ?
   Hear'st thou the groans that rend his breast ?

HIGHLAND MARY.

By *ARCHIBALD MUNRO.*

REPRINTED FROM THE "SCOTSMAN," OCTOBER 20, 1891.

THERE is probably no name in Scottish literature that has more tenderly touched the hearts of her countrymen than that of Mary Campbell. Though born of an obscure family, brought up in circumstances little fitted to attract general attention, and credited with no achievement that invests heroism with permanent or even temporary distinction, this Highland girl is a brilliant star in the galaxy of Fame, and has become the object of unmingled admiration. She died on the 20th of October, 1786. The lustre of Mary's name, like that of other stars and planets, borrows its fascination from a luminary brighter and greater than itself, and the very obscurity of her earlier condition enlarges by contrast the halo that now encircles her name. Moralists have lauded her virtues, critics have lovingly dropped their satiric shafts when commenting on her life, and poets have exhausted their resources in their effort to convey their conceptions of her excellence ; but all their contributions to the sum of her praise have taken their origin and complexion from the picture which inspired genius has given of her to the world. The interest created by the association of the heroine's career with that of the gifted lover who has procured for her the honour of poetical immortality is not, it is pleasant to know, confined to the country that gave her birth. In England, Ireland, America, and the Colonies her worth, unfortunate fate, and her premature death have found admirers and sympathisers as cordial and sincere as any that Caledonia has produced.

Of the particulars of the life of Mary we have but a very meagre account, and, curiously enough, it happens that in the locality where from first to last she passed most of her days little is known and still less recorded of her ; while the town where she spent but a few days of her existence has by the mere accident of her death there almost monopolised the attention of her biographers. Official documents, as well as consistent traditions, have assigned to Dunoon the honour of being her birthplace. Mary was born in the year 1768, in Auchamore or, by interpretation, Bigfield, a space of ground forming the south-western and south-eastern parts of Kirn and Dunoon respectively. A complete transforma-tion in the aspect of the district from what it was, as I remember fifty years ago, has, with other antique buildings overtaken the plain but interesting but-an'-ben, where Mary drew her first breath. The spirit of modern improvement is answerable for the disappearance of the notable cottage. Mary's father, who in the earlier years of his manhood was a seaman in a Revenue cruiser, bought and commanded a small sloop for the coal trade between Campbeltown, Troon, and other small ports on the Firth of Clyde. Finding the residence of his family at Dunoon to be inconvenient for all parties, he had them removed to Campbeltown. At the time of his migration, Mary, the eldest of his children, was nearly eight years of age ; and her unbroken connection with her new home extended over a little more than a similar number of years. Faithful to the instincts of clan-ships the Campbells took quarters in the immediate neighbourhood of one Elizabeth Campbell or M'Neill, a cousin of the head of the family. It is from Julia M'Neill,

a daughter of Elizabeth Campbell, that the later inquirers
into the history of Highland Mary, while resident in Campbeltown, have received whatever amount of information
existed there regarding her. In my early school days I
frequently saw Julia, as well as many others who were
personally acquainted with the whole of the family to which
Mary Campbell belonged. Mrs. M'Neill's house as well as
Mrs. Campbell's, stood in Broombrae at the head of Saddell
Street. It is only a few years since the tenement was
removed to make way for the present more substantial
erection.

According to Miss M'Neill's statement, which has been
corroborated by others who had knowledge of the case, Mary
Campbell was a great favourite with every one that knew
her—a distinction which she owed to her pleasant manners,
sweet temper, and obliging disposition. Her figure was
graceful ; the cast of her face was singularly delicate and of
fair complexion, and her eyes, which were bluish and lustrous
had a remarkably winning expression. The readers of the
brief account of her given by Burns's biographers are aware
that sincerity was a feature of the maiden, on which her
mother in after years used to dilate with peculiar compla-
cency ; and her school companions took special note of her
love of peace. Possessed of good natural abilities, and
faithful to her duties as a pupil, she was always able to gain
a prominent position in her class ; but should a dispute arise
at any time as to her right to occupy it, she was prepared to
surrender it with right goodwill in the interests of peace,
and to pacify the probably unreasonable disputant. This
spirit of conciliation was such a noticeable trait in her
character, and was so highly appreciated by her schoolmates
and others that, in accordance with the practice of the place,

where any one who is noted for qualities either good or bad, is known simply by his christian name, she came to be recognised by the distinction of "Mary" only. It may be mentioned, though a matter of course, that in a district at that period almost wholly Celtic, she was not known by the name of Highland Mary ; that distinction was reserved for another time and for a different locality. Liberality was also a ruling trait in Mary's character. Of the presents which her father was accustomed to bring home from the various ports he visited, his eldest child was sure to receive the most and best. These partial favours were offered her for, among other reasons, her assiduity and devotion to her mother in the discharge of domestic duties. It was not in the girl's power, however, to retain for her own use and pleasure the tokens of another's kindness to herself. Other hands than Mary's were often seen to handle and possess presents not originally intended for them. It thus became a common remark among the knowing ones of the neighbour-hood that Mary was too good for this world, and could not live long.

To the unutterable grief of the whole family it was arranged that she was to go to service in a household some-what distant from home. Her new sphere of duty was in Coilsfield or Montgomery Castle, in the immediate vicinity of Tarbolton, in the county of Ayr. For this position she was indebted to a Campbeltown lady, the celebrated Miss Arbuckle, who became by marriage a member of the Eglinton family. At the adjacent Parish Church of Tarbol-ton, Mary used to worship on Sundays with other members of the Coilsfield household, although her acquaintance with the English language was somewhat imperfect ; her pronun-ciation of it, indeed, was so tainted with the Gaelic accent that she soon obtained the more familiar name of Highland Mary. Other celebrities in Burns's diary, such as John Wilson, the whipper-in, Dr. Hornbook, James Humphrey, and John Lees, were numbered among the congregation that met in the Clachan Church. Burns, who resided in a farm almost equidistant from the kirks of Mauchline and Tarbolton, seems to have divided his Sabbaths between these kirks according to other considerations, as has been hinted, than the reputation of their preachers or the quality of their sermons. In the latter church, and shortly after her arrival, the poet saw the interesting young stranger, was charmed with her appearance and propriety of conduct, and was, of course, desirous of making her acquaintance. One of Mary's noticeable habits during the church service was a close attention to her Bible while the minister was reading from it, or referring to passages illustrative of his text. It has been conjectured that her loyal observance of this important duty may have suggested to the mind of the poet the exchange of Bibles which took place on a subsequent and memorable occasion.

There survived till very recently, in the neighbourhood of Montgomery Castle, an elderly and intelligent gentleman, who learned from a contemporary of the period the circumstances in which Burns sought and obtained an introduction to his new "fancy." In those days a pining swain might have an opportunity of unburdening his overweighted feelings towards the object of his regard by the aid of a blackfoot— a kind of official who could in many cases promote a crony's interests and attend to his own at the same time. In the course of a visit to his sweetheart, a blackfoot could secure her influence with a female fellow-servant to consent to a meeting with a companion of his who was sighing for an interview.

It was thus that Burns got the coveted introduction—a favour which his ready wit, his fascinating eyes, and impassioned eloquence improved to the utmost. It so happens that the individual who in early youth did such yeoman service to Burns in the capacity of blackfoot exercised in a later age his valuable talents in favour of the gentleman I have referred to. A series of extremely diverting incidents connected with the visits of Burns and of his guide, philosopher, and friend to their respective charmers were among the old gentleman's favourite reminiscences.

The intimacy between Burns and Mary ripened, as every record tells, into the tenderest bonds of mutual affection. At a distance of a few yards from the western side of the Castle, and close to the footpath, there was formerly a thorn tree, whose stem divided into three equally shaped branches and under whose ample shade the lovers were wont to meet. The tree was by turns called " Burns's Thorn " and " Mary's Tryst." The position of the thorn and the attitude of the lovers on a seat beneath its branches are well represented in the Caledonian Muse, compiled, edited, and published, within a dozen years after the poet's death, by Mr. George Thomson, his celebrated correspondent. The view of the thorn, the lovers, and the surrounding scenery is exceedingly pleasing. A few years ago the print in Mr. Thomson's own copy of the musical compilation, which was his own and Burns's joint production, was cut out of its venerable place and presented to me by his elder daughter, then in the 96th year of her age. A tree so affectingly associated with the courting days of Burns was sure to tempt the cupidity of the relic-hunter. For many years it was becoming small by degrees and beautifully less.

About a couple of hundreds yards up the River Faile, an affluent of the Ayr, and west from the thorn, there flows a small stream called the Alton, which joins the former river at the outskirts of the Coilsfield grounds. On the occasion of the final meeting between Burns and Mary, they are said to have stood on the opposite side of a stream, and then to have clasped hands after first laving them in the current, as a pledge of faithfulness to their vows of marriage. At the same time they exchanged Bibles, with appropriate inscriptions in them. The place where the Alton runs into the Faile would appear, from several considerations, to have been the scene of the remarkable ceremony thus enacted.

The Bible presented by Burns has, after crossing the Atlantic twice, and experiencing a singularly eventful career found its permanent resting-place in the monument on the banks of the Ayr. Fifty years ago, in consequence of the faint association of the lovers' names in the public mind, comparatively little notice was taken of the volumes, or of the precious autograph inscription with which they were assigned to Mary. Since that period, however, there has been, to my certain knowledge, a constantly increasing accession to the tribute of respect paid to her memory. The volumes in the monument are the first and most engrossing objects of attention and curiosity with visitors, and the last to re-engage their gaze as they retire. "Time but the impression stronger makes as streams their channels deeper wear." The only source of regret—and it is a keen one— which the visitor experiences on quitting the case where the volumes are exhibited, is the circumstance that Mary's similar gift to Burns is not seen beside them. What has become of that volume, with appropriate texts of Scripture inscribed by Mary's own hand, is a deep mystery and is likely to remain so. Not even that scrap of autograph survives her romantic career. What would not the lovers of romance and poetry give to have access to such a relic ! With regard to the extant volumes, it may be observed that a very remarkable change is taking place in the appearance of the poet's handwriting in them. Years ago the characters were clear and distinct, though delicate, as was the characteristic of his penmanship, generally, at the period when he wrote them ; but on recently inspecting them I was surprised and grieved to observe a very decided process of effacement going on. Some of the lighter turns and strokes are so obscure as scarcely to be legible. In the course of a few more years they will at this rate become altogether invisible. Such a consummation would be simply deplorable. The exhibition of the book without the exposure of the autograph should satisfy the public, in consideration of the gain that would be secured. On very important occasions the volumes might be opened for a short time. This course has been adopted in the case of a Burns book in the Mechanics' Library in Dumfries, and with excellent results—the letters seem to be regaining their former clearness.

• At the beginning of the autumn of 1786 Mary went to Campbeltown to make preparations for her contemplated change in life, and there remained till the beginning of October, when she returned to Greenock accompanied by her father. The correspondence that passed between her and her betrothed between August and October must have been of the most interesting character. What it was cannot now be known. To borrow a figure from one of the sports of the field, it may be said that the dews of the morning are past, and it is vain to continue the chase in meridan splendour. The letters received by Mary were religiously preserved by her, and afterwards affectionately treasured by her family. Many years later, however, when the poet's reputation declined, and taunts were hurled at the Campbells on account of their connection with him, Mary's elder brother got forcible possession of the priceless collection, and, amid the remonstrances and even the execrations of the rest of the household, committed it to the flames. The recent loss by some means or other of the box in which Mary stowed away her lover's letters has occasioned her few surviving relatives much regret, as it was the last relic they possessed.

Mary's tragic fate shortly after her return to Greenock is known to everybody. No intelligent and sympathetic emigrant or foreigner on a tour thinks of quitting the old country without paying a visit to her hallowed grave. The adjoining kirk, which all but claims Dr. Chalmers as one of her ministers, is well patronised in summer ; and the strangers who worship there exchange, on leaving its precincts, one sacred site for the other.

To-day, the 20th of October, is the anniversary of the heroine's death, as well as of the date of its commemoration by our national bard ; and such is the importance that has been attached to both the event and its poetical record, that at the request of a late popular biographer, an eminent professor of astronomy worked out and supplied a scientific confirmation of the correctness of the assumed date of their connection. The brilliant planet that at present nightly illumes our southern sky suggests the occasion on which the poet apostrophised the "star that ushered in the day his Mary from his soul was torn." It was thus that a lovely phenomenon in the heavens combined with fancy's meteor ray to perpetuate the name and fame of gentle Highland Mary.

CONCERNING HIGHLAND MARY.

By REV. WILLIAM WYE SMITH.

ANYONE who has gone by the Canadian Pacific Railway, from Toronto to Owen Sound, will remember the great "Horse-shoe" bend, a few miles south of Orangeville. Almost immediately at the top of this bend, the train passes under a wooden bridge ; and a quarter of a mile farther north, under a slender iron one. This iron bridge is on the farm of William Anderson ; and among the hills, a few rods west of the Railway, are his farm-buildings, and the stone house he built with his own hands. He is dead now ; and his children occupy the farm. He was the son of the only sister of MARY CAMPBELL, Burns's "Highland Mary!"

The township of *Caledon* is wondrously hilly and stony. Hilly it will always be ; but many of the stones are being gathered off. I had been staying overnight with the late John Brown, in the western part of the township. Brown, who had shouldered a gun for Mackenzie in the Rebellion of 1837, though too late to join in the fray near Toronto, was a lineal descendant of John Brown the carrier, inhumanly slain by Claverhouse. I walked over from his place, on the last day of the year 1885, across the little Credit River, and among the hills for a few miles eastward, to visit the relatives of Highland Mary. The railway bowls along through a gully, a few yards east of the house, in its endeavour to rise from the Lake Ontario to the Lake Huron level. I had passed over the railway frequently, since its opening some years ago ; and had I known of a nephew of Highland Mary's there, I should have visited him. His

2

daughter, and two sons, live on the farm. Another son, married, lives a mile north. A fourth son is in California.

Antiquarian research, like many other things, takes hold of a man who gives himself to it. And perhaps these good people wondered at my being so interested in their family history, and inquiring so anxiously for any relics they might possess of their famous kinswoman. The relic of relics which they once possessed, had been parted with, and was in Scotland—Burns's Bible, in two volumes; in one of which had been placed by the hands of her mother, a long lock of MARY's golden hair. They had nothing now, but some photographs of their father, and others of the family connection. Some of these they loaned me for copying. They lived in a plain storey-and-a-half stone farm-house, on an exceedingly hilly farm, on the " Caledon mountain."

The stranger was made welcome, with a hospitality in-herited with their Highland blood, with which people it is a cardinal virtue—and yet his business had to be plainly stated, in tribute to the Lowland caution, which came in with the blood of the ANDERSON's. I staid all night, and had a New Year's dinner with them, before the elder brother brought me through the romantic valley of the Credit River, and up the " mountain " on the other side, in a buggy, to old John Brown's again.

The dislike which the father of Highland Mary, Archibald Campbell, had to Burns, has not come down to his des-cendants. These estimable people doted on everything connected with Burns and Highland Mary—their grand-mother having been Mary's only sister, ANNIE ; and they told me all they knew, (and got from me all I knew), on the subject. Yet I found I was only on the threshold of my researches ; and that I had yet to get hold of the historian of the family connection—some one person, who either by natural gift or surrounding circumstances, possesses the whole history, and all the antiquarian lore of the race. I think I found the right person afterwards ; yet the information and traditions, reposing now with the third generation, and unguided by documentary statements, are becoming thin and attenuated, and fast fading away. And though, on the whole, I have met with unexpected success in my researches, I only wish they had been made twenty years sooner, to be just so much the better !

Burns only mentions any particulars about Highland Mary in his correspondence once. And that is all we know from Burns respecting her, except that he seemed very down-hearted one night, and told John Blaine, the hired man, that " Mary had refused to meet him."

Mary Campbell was a native of the district of Cowal, being born near Dunoon, on the Firth of Clyde. She was born in a thatched cottage, not now standing, on the farm of Auchamore, in the parish of Dunoon. The date of her birth cannot now be recovered. She was the eldest of eight children, only three of whom lived to grow up. The safest conjecture we can make, is to assume she was twenty three at the time of her death in 1786. On the 19th June, 1762, " Archibald Campbell, in Daling, and Agnes Campbell, in Auchamore, gave in their names to be proclaimed to marriage." So reads an old parish record, unearthed three years ago. In her childhood, Mary lived some time at Loch Ranza, in Arran, with a minister, who was a relative of her mother's. It is not known by the present descendants of Mary's parents, whether they were related or not by blood.

The father was a sailor. At some time, by some accident, he had lost an eye. A correspondent of mine, Mr. Matthew

Turnbull of Rothesay, tells me the old man used an eye-glass,
which is now in his possession—as also a needle-book of
Highland Mary's. Mr. Turnbull's wife, now deceased, was
a granddaughter of the old sailor. A grandson of the old
pair, so late as 1886, in a deposition says, " My grandfather
and grandmother removed from Dunoon to Campbeltown
after all their children were born. He traded between
Troon and Campbeltown. From the way my grandmother
spoke, I think my grandfather owned the smack himself."
Other authorities, however, state very positively that at the
date of Mary's death, he was on a Revenue cutter, stationed
at Campbeltown. The old people afterwards lived at
Greenock, and died there.

Mary had been induced by a relative of the family, Mrs.
Isabella Campbell (who herself had lived in Ayrshire), to
come to that county, and take a situation as a servant. It
is tolerably certain that she was at one time in the family of
Gavin Hamilton, BURNS's friend ; and there probably there the
poet first saw her. At the time of their parting (14th May,
1786,) she seemed to be dairymaid at Col. Hugh Montgomerie's (afterward Earl of Eglintoune), at Coilsfield,
poetically named by Burns "The Castle o' Montgomerie."
Robert Chambers gives us some information as to the *date*
of this acquaintance. The late Sir Daniel Wilson, of
Toronto University, tells me that *he* obtained much of this
information from Chambers. Together they make out that
it was at the darkest hour of the Poet's history, when Jean
Armour had cast him off. Others turned from him, but
MARY had faith in him, and was willing to take him " for
better or for worse," and to go with him to the West Indies
(whither he had now determined to sail), or to await his return after a lapse of perhaps some years. Allan Cunning-

ham says, "On the day of their separation, they plighted
their mutual faith by the exchange of Bibles. They stood,
with a running stream between them [the Burn 'Faile'],
and lifting up water in their hands, vowed to love while
woods grew and water ran!" It was a wooded secluded
spot on the north bank of the Ayr. I have a painting of it,
in oil, by a young friend, before me as I write. Burns's
pledge was a pocket Bible in two volumes, rather elegantly
bound. Thousands from America have seen them on the
banks of the Doon. Mary's present was a plainer copy in
one volume.

Burns's muse at this time was constant and musical. In
April, shortly before he parted with Mary, he wrote "The
Mountain Daisy." Also, about the same time, "The
Lament," and "Despondency," and "To Ruin," and the
song, "Again Rejoicing Nature Sees." And in that month
of May itself, he wrote the finest of all his poetical
"epistles," that to young Andrew Aitken—

> " I lang hae thought, my youthfu' friend,
>   A something to have sent you ;
> Though it should serve no other end
>   Than just a kind memento.
> But how the subject-theme may gang,
>   Let time and chance determine ;
> Perhaps it may turn out a sang,
>   Perhaps turn out a sermon ! " . . .

Of the history of that summer of 1786, as far as regards
MARY, little is known. Mary was the eldest of the family.
Two brothers living—one of whom died that autumn—and
one only sister, Annie. Annie's birth, as I have it from her
husband's family-bible, dates 1st March, 1774 : she was

therefore, when Mary parted from Burns, and came home
to get her parents' consent, and prepare for her marriage,
twelve years old.

The family must have been poor. The very fact of Mary
going out to domestic service, when, as the eldest of the
children, her services would be so valuable to her mother,
may be held, I think, to satisfactorily settle the question.
A mother will not send her only helper away, except when
poverty makes it necessary.

The father was still in middle age, firm and unyielding ;
and, unfortunately, just as ready to stick to a prejudice as
to a principle. He took a dislike to BURNS, which, under
all the circumstances, is not to be wondered at. But he
carried the prejudice so far as to *burn* everything connected
with BURNS which he found among his daughter's papers
and belongings after her death. Mr. Turnbull, the surviving son-in-law of Annie Campbell, writes me, "My
wife told me, *there were a* GREAT MANY THINGS *burned.*"
Burns's bible was spared just because it *was* a bible. A
Scotsman will not burn a *bible.* An old relative of mine,
having a bible too ragged for further use, reverently buried
it in the "kirkyard." He would not burn it.

Though BURNS never once at this time mentioned Mary
in his letters to others, nor apparently to his mother's
household at Mossgiel, it is quite certain to me that he
wrote, and frequently, to MARY. Miss Mary Anderson,
who by her marriage became Mrs. Kilgour (formerly of Ayr,
Ontario, and now of Chicago), tells me that her grandmother,
Mary's sister, used to sing to her children pieces of songs
which BURNS *had written in his letters to Mary.* Poor girl ;
she had none to sympathise with her : her parents did not
want to hear anything of BURNS ; and what so natural as

that she should make a confidant of sister Annie—the only
sister she had—she a fair-haired gilpie of twelve years old ?
or that she should teach Annie to sing the songs which, no
doubt, she sang herself ?

"These songs," writes Mrs. Kilgour, "*were never in
print*: although William Anderson [the Canadian emigrant
and possessor of Burns's *bibles*] had given some of the songs
he had heard his mother sing to WILLIAM MOTHERWELL,
who was collecting all he could in regard to Burns's Poems,
for a work he was busy with then. But he died before it
was ready to be published, so the songs were never printed."
So writes my fair friend in Chicago.

I have been unable to recover anything of this nature
from the papers of William Anderson, now in possession of
his family. As soon as I got the above information from
Mrs. Kilgour, I again visited " Caledon Mountain," and
spent another night at the Andersons'. But they assured
me that they had looked over all that their father had left
behind him, dozens of times, and that there were no memor-
andum books nor manuscripts—nothing in the shape of
"papers" at all, except three or four letters from his
brothers and sisters in Scotland. Why don't people write
down what they don't want to forget ?

Mrs. Kilgour writes me, that when Motherwell visited
her mother's house (she herself was then a wee toddling
thing), the Poet asked " What MARY looked like ? " and
" What colour was her hair ? " Her mother answered " Her
hair was *just like that bairn's.*" And asking the mother's
leave, he severed a little ringlet from the child's head, and
put it reverently in his waistcoat pocket.

A thousand pities hang around the story—that the correspondence drawn out by the purest and most romantic of

BURNS's attachments should have been burned by a preju-
diced father ; and that the snatches of songs Mary had confided to her young and only sister, and treasured up in the
memory of her son, should be also apparently entirely lost.
    The summer of 1786 passed away.   BURNS was busy in
the end of June, and all July, in copying poems, and cor-
recting proofs, and obtaining subscribers.   On 31st July,
612 copies of the book were issued at Kilmarnock, he having
secured between three and four hundred subscribers.   And
he was now preparing to sail for the West Indies.
    Robert Chambers says, " There is no evidence that Mary
had taken any steps in arranging matters for a union with
BURNS, though it is believed that she received letters from
him." I have satisfactory evidence that Chambers's belief with
regard to BURNS writing letters is correct.   Her father was
bitterly opposed to the marriage.   Mary is held on all hands
by her relatives to have been the most gentle and amiable
of maidens.   From what Chambers says, immediately following, the conclusion seems extremely probable that the
marriage was postponed in the meantime, at least till
BURNS should see how matters would go with him in the
West Indies.   And all such arrangements must have been
made by correspondence.   Chambers in his researches,
learned that Mary, at the recommendation of the same relative who had introduced her to service in Ayrshire, had
agreed to accept a new situation, for "a term," in the
family of Col. M'Ivor, of Glasgow.
    BURNS expressly says, she crossed the sea to meet him ;
(from Campbeltown to Greenock).   We may suppose she was
on her way to her new place in Glasgow, and said nothing
of BURNS to her father, when she accompanied him to
Greenock.   His principal errand was to bring his boy

Robert, who was to enter upon his apprenticeship with
Peter Macpherson, a ship-carpenter, who was a cousin of
Mrs. Campbell's. The father himself in after years, is described in some document, as a "ship-carpenter in Greenock."
In accordance with the convivial habits of the time, a
" Brothering Feast " was held in the house of Macpherson,
as a welcome and initiation of the new Brother-Craftsman.
Robert felt unwell the next day. Mary jocularly observed
that " he had probably taken a little too much after supper "
the night before. Macpherson, to keep up the badinage said
jokingly, " O then, it is just as well, in case of the worst,
that I have agreed to purchase that *lair* in the kirk-yard ! "
This otherwise unimportant bit of pleasantry, enables us to
fix, within a very few days, the date of Mary's death ; for
Chambers discovered the date of the purchase thus alluded
to by Macpherson.

Robert's illness proved very serious ; and Mary nursed
him through it. Somewhere, in the mist of years gone by,
I have seen quoted the remark of Mrs. Macpherson, that
among her children, "Mary was like an Angel in the house !"
Doubtless so !

In a few days, as Robert got better, MARY took ill. Her
illness was soon declared to be a fever of a malignant type,
then prevalent in the town ; and in a few days the poor girl
died. I have anxiously enquired of all the descendants of
her sister, if she said anything of BURNS, or left any messages
for him on her deathbed ? They all say they never heard of
her so doing. And then it must be remembered that in
fevers of this class, the head is generally much affected.
The poor heart ceased to beat ; with all its hopes and secrets
undivulged to those who had no sympathy with them ! She
was buried in the "lair" Macpherson had so recently bought,

being the first of the family connection who was placed in it.
There was then no registry of deaths or burials in the parish.
But the transfer of the burial-plot to Macpherson from
Duncan Robertson, bears date Oct. 12, 1786. BURNS says
Mary died at "the close of the autumn." In Scotland
(different from the reckoning in America), "autumn" begins
with August, and ends with October.

The grave is in the burial-ground of the West Kirk, close
to the Firth. Near the west end is Macpherson's burial-
plot. Here, in 1842, some admirers of BURNS erected a tall
elegant sculptured structure over the remains of HIGHLAND
MARY. It contains a sculpture representing the parting of
the lovers, surmounted by a figure weeping over an urn, on
which is inscribed the name "MARY." Mr. Matthew
Turnbull, whom I have mentioned as son-in-law of Annie
Campbell, sends me the following, as the inscription on
Highland Mary's tomb, copied by him at my request :—

" ERECTED
OVER THE GRAVE OF HIGHLAND MARY,
1842.

My Mary, dear departed shade,
Where is thy place of blissful rest ? "

Mary's age, and the date of her death, are not given on
the monument; for the reason that they have not been
exactly ascertained. Mr. Turnbull tells me that Mary's
father and mother are buried in the same plot.

Spending a night with Alexander M'Lachlan, the Scotch
Canadian poet, we were speaking on the congenial subject of
BURNS ; and he told me he had, like many another pilgrim,
visited the grave of HIGHLAND MARY, at Greenock. He

said he did not greatly admire the monument—but there was one thing that *did* greatly draw his attention—and that was, a *well-beaten path*, that led to the grave; *and ended there!* Trodden by the feet of countless pilgrims, to whom the West Kirk is nothing—and Greenock is nothing—only as they contain the dust of HIGHLAND MARY! How many hearts have echoed the thought—

> If on this earth there is a spot
> To which my soul admiring turns,
> It is the Land of Walter Scott,
> It is the Land of Robert Burns!
> Oh for a glimpse of that proud Land,
> Where Genius all triumphant shines!
> To stray a pilgrim, staff in hand,
> And worship at her thousand shrines!

Three years after Mary's death, (on the very anniversary of her decease,) BURNS penned his immortal ode, "To Mary in Heaven." His wife, wondering that he did not come in for his evening meal, found him, where in the Autumn gloaming he had flung himself down in the stackyard, gazing at the evening star, entirely oblivious to everything around. *He* shortly after came in; and going straight to his desk, wrote down as if from memory, "To Mary in Heaven."

On 14th November, 1792, from Dumfries, he writes to Mr. George Thomson, publisher, Edinburgh, as follows :—

MY DEAR SIR,—I agree with you that the song *Catherine Ogie* is very poor stuff, altogether unworthy of so beautiful an air. I tried to amend it; but the awkward sound *Ogie* recurring so often in the rhyme spoils every attempt at introducing sentiment into the piece. The foregoing song (Highland Mary,) pleases myself; I think it is in my happiest manner ; you will see at first glance that it suits the air. The subject of the song is one of the most interesting passages of my youthful days, and I own that I should be much flattered to see the verses set to an air which would ensure celebrity. Perhaps, after all, 'tis the still glowing prejudice of my heart that throws a borrowed lustre over the merits of the composition.

Of other effusions of his Muse, relating to Mary Campbell, "My Highland Lassie, O," is avowed by BURNS to relate to her. It has some sweet lines, and breathes a fine spirit. It is less known, and less used, than it deserves to be. This song was evidently written in 1786. "Will ye go to the Indies, my Mary?" was also written at this time. The poem "Powers Celestial, whose Protection," was named by BURNS himself, "A Prayer for Mary."

The beautiful song "Afton Water," Gilbert Burns (his brother, and to a large extent his confident,) tells us was composed by Burns on his long and dearly-loved HIGHLAND MARY : that BURNS *told him so!* There is no possible reason for doubting Gilbert Burns's truth and reliability in the matter ; and very little for supposing he might be mistaken. And though the song is attributed by most of BURNS's editors—following Dr. Currie, who probably had his information from the household at Dumfries—to a desire on BURNS's part to compliment Mrs. Stewart of Afton Lodge, until I get better proof, I choose to follow Gilbert Burns, that the Poet wrote it in honour of his long-loved and ever-remembered HIGHLAND MARY. I recall no other of BURNS's heroines on whom he lavished, not two, three, nor four—but SIX immortal poems : two of them the sublimest and tenderest love-pieces that ever were written !

One of the minor blessings of our own day is the art of

Photography. None now so poor but they may carry with them a likeness of those they love. Vastly different was it a hundred years ago ; and, as may be supposed, no likeness exists of HIGHLAND MARY. Sir Noel Paton's painting of " Highland Mary " is, I conclude, wholly a "fancy " portrait ; as none of the connections of Mary Campbell know anything of any relative ever " sitting " for it.

For years and years—ever from a boy—dreaming in the shade, or on some maple bank, or fishing in some nameless stream—I wondered " If ever I could write anything like BURNS ? " or " What Highland Mary looked like ? " and I am glad I can give something of an answer to the latter question. I have a photograph of Mary Anderson, Annie Campbell's eldest daughter, whom she named after her sister MARY, (Highland Mary,) and who was said by everybody to be " the perfect picture " of her celebrated namesake. But there was no photography in her youth ; and she was perhaps forty-five when the picture was taken ; and so I managed to further obtain a photograph of Margaret Robertson, her daughter, who was young—and in her turn a perfect image of her mother. And she, though one generation further away—being a grand-niece of HIGHLAND MARY— presents the best likeness the world has yet seen of Highland Mary ; *and all we shall ever have!* And we are thankful for that much ! I am proud and happy to have been able to do even this.

Annie, Mary Campbell's only sister, married on 6th August, 1792, at Greenock, when she was 18, (Burns was then living in Dumfries,) Mr. James Anderson, a young stone-mason. He died at Renton, 23rd March, 1823, aged 62. His wife died 23rd January, 1824. Annie Campbell

(Mrs. Anderson) had, like her mother, two daughters ; and
like her she named them " Mary " and " Annie."

On the point of the niece resembling the aunt, I present
the testimony of all Annie Campbell's descendants. And I
present the distinct testimony of Mr. Matthew Turnbull, of
Rothesay, who married the younger of Annie Campbell's
daughters. In answer to my question, " Did Mrs. Robertson (Mary Anderson) resemble Highland Mary 1 " his answer
was, [I quote from his letter,] " *She was said to be very like
her*, and was called after her." " Was Mrs. Turnbull [his
own wife] like her aunt 1 " Mr. Turnbull very candidly
answered, " It was said, *No*."

The Andersons are a handsome race. We would all be
pleased to think that MARY CAMPBELL, their relative, was a
beautiful girl, with pale golden hair, and sparkling blue eyes
—the personification of modest worth and womanly affection.
And it is not all fancy to say so, and believe it. Through
the dreamy melancholy of the face of her niece and namesake, Mary Anderson (Mrs. Robertson,)—who had domestic
sorrows of her own, poor woman—we think we can discover
a shadow of what MARY must have been ; and in Margaret
Robertson's picture we have doubtless a close presentation
of the face of BURNS's heroine. A copy of this picture which
I sent to the late Dr. Charles Rogers, was placed by him in
the Kilmarnock Monument, among the other relics and
mementos of BURNS. All through the family-connection
runs the full rounded chin, with a slight dimple ; long,
rather than short—reminding one of the Empress Eugenie.
A rather long straight nose ; the classical rounded jaw ; the
peculiar eyelids, folding down over the eyes with no wrinkles
at the corners, and with scarcely a crease ; the fair hair,
combatting the darker Anderson tint, even in the third

generation ; and the flashing of the eye—seen in Margaret
Robertson's picture. It is all the world will ever know of
HIGHLAND MARY's face !

Mrs. Kilgour writes me from Chicago, " My mother, if
she had been alive, would have been able to give you a great
deal in regard to Mary Campbell. It is only what I can remember hearing her say that I know. Highland Mary was
rather tall—fair complexion—light yellow hair—blue eyes—
quite retired— of gentle, amiable disposition."

Mr. Turnbull writes, in answer to my enquiries about
HIGHLAND MARY's personal appearance, that " Her complexion was fair—reddish ; " eyes blue. Of her hair, he says
the long lock of pale gold in the Monument at the Doon has
changed a little since it left his house, now near 60 years
ago. Hair does fade. He says also that Mrs. Robertson's
hair " was said to be quite like it."

Mrs. Campbell got over her dislike to BURNS sooner than
did her husband—who probably never changed. BURNS
visited the family, probably only the once but the mother
had not quite " come round." He begged some memento of
his lost love—" a handkerchief," or anything ; but the
mother refused, though he asked it with tears streaming
down his face !

But the old woman lived to think better of him ; and
even to sing the song of " Highland Mary," and others in
which he had celebrated his Highland lassie.

Chambers says, when she was asked " If she thought MARY
would have been happy with BURNS, if she had lived ? "
She " thought her sweet lassie could never have been happy
with so wild and profane a man as BURNS." But she would
immediately add, as she remembered the visit he had paid
her, " But he was a *real warm-hearted chiel !* "

The same authority says, '' The old woman always spoke
of MARY, who was the eldest of her children, as a paragon of
gentleness and amiability.   Her *sincerity* was a quality,
which above all others, the mother fondly dwelt on.''

The stern old sailor seemed never to have changed his
mind on the subject of BURNS ; and his two sons, to some
extent at least, shared his prejudices.   It is believed, by the
present members of the family, that one of the brother's
erased BURNS's name from one volume of the Bible he had
given MARY.

We have, many of us, lived in '' Arcadia ; '' and our observation has shown us that fathers are apt to be far more
exacting with a lover, and every way harder to please, where
an eldest daughter is involved, than when there has already
been a wedding or two in the household.   And the old
sailor of Campbeltown was, I suppose, no exception, and
resented probably the idea of *anybody* '' takin' awa *his*
lassie ! ''   But it was quite different with the sister.   She
fondly clung to the memory of the loved and lost one ; and
while she had her, sympathized with her feelings.   Mrs.
Kilgour writes me, '' Mary's sister Annie was very fond of
her, and spoke of her as being so gentle and mild ; and did
not seem herself to share the rest of the family's dislike to
BURNS.''

MARY herself was probably a singer.   Her mother sang,
and her sister ; and Mary, that summer at home, was often,
no doubt, heard lilting about the house some of RAB's sangs !

The Andersons have told me that their grandmother,
MARY's sister, left a Gaelic Bible.   As a rule, people do not
keep Gaelic Bibles who are unable to read them.   And if
she could read and speak Gaelic, it is still more certain that
her elder sister MARY could do the same ; especially as we

remember that some of her early years were spent in the family of a Gaelic minister in Arran.

Now, our universal experience is, that the speaking of Gaelic has an effect on the pronunciation of English, as spoken by the same person. I had an old lady friend, who generally went once a year to Beaverton, on Lake Simcoe, to visit some Highland relatives for a month. And she told me how her fashionable daughters would laugh at her *English* for some weeks after her return. The Gaelic had spoiled, for the time, her English!

And there is little doubt that in MARY's speech there would be a little softening of some of the English vocables. These little peculiarities, marking her as a stranger in Ayrshire, would (without necessarily any disparagement whatever being intended by the term) be quite sure to suggest the name, "Highland Mary," as a convenient way of distinguishing her, where there would be so many "Maries." "Margaret" is the most common name in Scotland ; "Mary" comes next. It is not necessary to suppose "Burns" invented the name ; he would find it ready to his hand, as a pet-name for his bright-eyed, bright-haired girl—and glorified the name !

Mr. Turnbull tells me, that some years before her death, Mary's mother gave a volume of BURNS's bible to each of her two grand-daughters, Mary and Annie Anderson. In one of them was a long lock of pale golden hair, which the mother had treasured since MARY's death in 1786. She said to the girls, "When you come to be married, you can sell these for as much as will get each of you a *Chest of Drawers !*" The girls were both married in 1828 ; Mary in April, and my correspondent and Annie on 19th August. Shortly before, their brother, William Anderson, had

3

persuaded them to sell *him* the volumes (with the lock of
hair) for £5 to each of them ; promising " they should never
go out of the Anderson family." And my correspondent
had it from his wife, that but for that *promise,* he would
never have got them.

When James Anderson's household was broken up, by his
death and the daughters' marriages, in 1828, William
Anderson boarded for two years with Mr. and Mrs. Turnbull : and in 1832 sailed to America. Before he went away,
Mr. Turnbull, (so he informs me) offered him £15 or £20
for the " Highland Mary " relics : but he chose to retain
them, and carried them with him over the sea. He was a
mason, and a little forehanded in the way of money. His
sister, Mrs. Turnbull, sewed 200 sovereigns in a belt for him
before he sailed. On the same vessel was another young
man, who after made his mark in Montreal, as an eminent
printer and publisher, Mr. John C. Beckett. The tedium
of a five or six weeks' passage would be relieved by many a
tale of the old Land, and the friends they had left behind ;
and the story of " BURNS's Bibles " was duly confided to
Mr. Beckett. In those days of big steamships, a steerage-
passenger's chests and heavy luggage are put down the hold,
and only what is in immediate use allowed to be retained
beside him. But then it was different : the young men
would each have his well-filled chest beside him : and the
precious *bibles,* and the long lock of hair, would be cautiously
produced.

The proverb that " A young man from the Old Country
never does well till his *Old Country money* is done ! " was
for the many thousandth time verified in William Anderson.
He wandered about Canada and the United States till his
money was nearly all gone ; and then settled on a " bush "

farm in the township of Caledon, 40 miles N.W. of Toronto. There were a good many Scotsmen in the Bush, here and there, around him ; and they must all see "Highland Mary's Bibles !" And one and another begged, till he had not the heart to refuse, "just the smallest possible bit " of the long lock of golden hair.

At length he "came to his last two-and-sixpence "—so he stated himself. Then the temptation occurred to him— fortified with the observation that the Bibles were becoming somewhat worn with so much handling, and the lock of hair growing somewhat less—of disposing of them in such a way, that while the money would do him good, the world might see them. His children have anxiously asked me " If the Bibles seemed *much worn*, when I saw them at Doon ?" I was glad to be able to tell them that the relics were in excellent preservation, and that the long lock of golden hair was intact, and likely to satisfy the eyes of generations yet to come.

William Anderson wrote to his friend and connection (for his brother, Robert, had married Beckett's sister) asking Mr. Beckett's advice in the matter. Mr. R. A. Beckett, of Montreal, writes me :—

" Mr. Anderson expended most of his money clearing his farm and making a home. And the *Bibles*, being the only valuables left, he proposed to sell, though very loath to do so. But as money was of more value to him at the time, he made up his mind to part with his treasures. So he wrote to my father (Mr. John C. Beckett) asking his advice. In answer to that letter, my father, with Mr. Rollo Campbell, Mr. Weir, the then editor of the *Montreal Herald*, with some few other Scotsmen, bought the Bibles for the sum of one hundred dollars. He was assured that the relics would be carefully treasured. They were sent to the Provost of Ayr, for the use of the public ; and on 24th December, 1840, were formally presented to Provost Tamond, for the relic-chamber of the Doon Monument, where they are to be seen at the present time. They were placed therein, on the Poet's Birthday, 25th January, 1841, at a Public Dinner given on the above date, in the Burns' Arms Hotel."

Mr. Turnbull of Rothesay, says :—"William Anderson wrote us, for two or three years after he left ; but stopped after that, for a long time. The first we heard of him, was when we heard of the *Bibles* being at Ayr ; and the wife and I went to Ayr, to see if it were really they—as we could not believe it was, after what he had said before he left. But we knew them as soon as we saw them ; which satisfied us."

I was sorry to have him say, in one of his letters to me, "I am now in my 79th year (this was in 1886,) and have forgotten what I used to hear of Highland Mary." Once more—why don't people write down what they don't want to forget ?

Here I leave the story. I would tell more, if I had discovered more. A visit to Scotland would, no doubt, have added some few particulars ; but even without it, I trust I may have interested those who linger over everything connected with BURNS and HIGHLAND MARY with fond and doting recollection.

Perhaps there never was an artless maid, about whom so little is known, who has inspired so deep a feeling in the hearts of her countrymen everywhere. And it was her faith in God—her faith in what was best in human nature—her perfect sincerity, and purity of character—her *loveableness,* and her power of loving—that draw all hearts to love her !

St. Catharines, Ontario.

HIGHLAND MARY.

Inscribed to JOHN D. ROSS, Esq.,

AUTHOR OF "SCOTTISH POETS IN AMERICA," EDITOR OF
"ROUND BURNS'S GRAVE," "BURNSIANA," etc.

FAIR flower who gav'st thy leal heart to the Bard
   That oft in noblest lays of thee has sung
   Melodious as thine own soft Gaelic tongue,
And cherished thee with sacredest regard.
Pure as the sparkling dew on beauteous rose,
   And chaste as snow on lofty Cruachan's brow
   Thy name and fame ; an influence good wert thou
That breathed sweet fragrance after thy life's close.
His hymn divine to thy " departed shade "
   Poured forth that memorable Autumn morn,
   The day thou wert from his fond bosom torn,
Lives soul-inspired and never shall it fade.
The ghoul who thy name hallowed dare defame
Should read the hymn, then melt in burning shame.

        DUNCAN MACGREGOR CRERAR.

AT THE TOMB OF HIGHLAND MARY.

By COLIN RAE BROWN.

IT is the great privilege of men whose names and works are immortal to have immortalised those also with whom they have been most intimately associated. We rarely speak of Dante without mentioning his Beatrice. The name of Petrarch seldom crosses our lips without that of Laura being also spoken. And while the universal fame of Burns lives enrolled upon the annals of everlasting memory, Highland Mary can never die—can never be forgotten. Side by side with that of Scotland's Ploughman Poet, her name will stand emblazoned upon the time-stained scroll of immortality. And why not? Had there been no Highland Mary, would not the grand heart utterings, the sweet soul-moving sentiments which she alone inspired, have remained unwritten? Should we ever have read that perhaps most beautiful of odes addressed to " Highland Mary ? "—have ever been moved to tears by those nobly passionate lines " To Mary in Heaven ? " which fall upon you like the wailing of the saddened soul from which they were wrung. Love is the grand-parent of Genius. Love begets inspiration ; inspiration begets Genius. We can never begrudge, then, the honour, the fame, and the immortality which belongs by right to those by whom the great are inspired.

"To HIGHLAND MARY."

" Oh, Mary ! dear departed shade ;
Where is thy place of blissful rest ? "

A few days ago I read these words, wrought in plain black letters upon the simple monument of white stone erected in the Old West Kirkyard at Greenock to the memory of her to whom Burns was dear. As I stood there, with the evening shadows falling around me, amid the time-worn tombs, whose inscriptions were, in many instances, almost wholly obliterated, my thoughts momentarily wandered away. They took me back to that hour in which I had been first able to read and understand for myself. They dwelt for the space of a few seconds upon the old green-covered volume of his poems I had then used—upon the thumb-marked, dog-eared page containing those verses which had been, and always would be, my favourite duet—

> " Ye banks and braes and streams around
>   The Castle o' Montgomery "—

and so on. How well I know every word of that poem? As my thoughts returned, and I felt my feet pressing the sod under which lay the dust of her by whom they were inspired, the concluding lines—immortal in˙ the very grandeur of their simplicity—rose instinctively to my lips—

> " Oh, pale, pale now those rosy lips
>   I oft hae kissed sae fondly !
> And closed for aye the sparkling glance
>   That dwelt on me sae kindly ;
> And mouldering now in silent dust
>   That heart that lo'ed me dearly !
> But still within my bosom's core
>   Shall live my Highland Mary."

With these words green in our memory, have we not an excuse for asking ourselves whether the life of Robert Burns,

whether its end would not have been different had Highland
Mary lived ?   Have we not a reason for believing that of all
his "attachments," this one was the purest, the most
sincere, and the most durable ?   Of a notoriously suscep-
tible nature, the poet was easily impressed.   In his general
admiration for the beautiful, as represented in either the
female mind or form, he was doubtlessly, oftentimes carried
away.   But to be impressed, infatuated, carried away, is not
to love with so great a sincerity, such a depth of passion as
alone could call forth such lines as I have quoted.   The
following description of the sweet dairymaid of Coilsfield is
taken from a well-known and excellent authority :—

"But superior in modesty and intelligence to the women
he had hitherto known, her character must have commanded
his respect as well as his love."

Respect and Love.   Are they not twin sisters ?   Must
they not ever go hand in hand ?   Can one die and the other
remain ?   Let us ask ourselves those questions almost in the
same breath as we ask whether Burns respected all the
women he had known prior to his meeting with Mary
Campbell ?   Even if she had lived, do we doubt for one
single shadow of a moment, that he would have married
Jean Armour, though legally not bound to do so ?   No ?
Robert Burns's honour was not such as was measured out
in the scales of legal responsibility, but in those of moral
conviction.

He would have married Jean Armour ; yes !—but would
she have been the beacon, the guiding star to warn him from
the rocks of destruction, against which he was wont to drift ?
While Highland Mary lived, would not hers have been the
imaginary hand that, with its soft, gentle, though firm,
touch, would have deterred and checked him in those
moments of wild and reckless impetuosity ?

When she died, when that hand was cold—

" And closed for aye the sparkling glance "—

the young sweet being crushed out in the very springtime of its existence, was not the nature of Burns just such an one as would chafe and grow restless and heedless under the cruel and untimely fate that had torn his "Highland Mary" from earth ? But did his love die—did not his heart still call, his eyes still look up through a mist of tears, " To Mary in Heaven ? "

BURNS AND HIGHLAND MARY.

By ROBERT REID.

A ROYAL harp hung in Life's palace hall ;
  And one by one, as out and in they strayed,
  The careless guests a fitful music made—
Striking its strings : so true the sounds did fall
That whoso heard straightway for more did call ;
  Thus many strains the willing harp essayed
  As many hands (and some unworthy !) played.
Ah ! but when Love, the master player of all,
  Parting in tears from one fair visitor,
Taught her deft fingers 'mong its cords to twine,—
  The poor dumb instrument, whose soul did stir
With sudden transport,—left on earth to pine,—
  Yearn'd evermore for the dear hands of her,
Knowing their touch t' have been indeed divine !

HIGHLAND MARY IN MARBLE.

By GEORGE SAVAGE.

A LIFE-SIZE statue of Mary Campbell stands in the Lennox Gallery, in the City of New York. The sculptor's skilful hand has unfolded from purest marble Mary Campbell, as lovely in form and features doubtless as was the Highland maiden Burns knew and loved. In her hands she clasps the Bible Burns gave her ; with downcast eyes, as if in maiden bashfulness, she looks into the clear depths of the fast flowing stream which separated them on that beautiful Sunday in May when they parted forever, and a Scottish plaid falls gracefully from her head and shoulders. It is a triumph of Art, in which Sculpture is wedded to Poetry and Love.

It was indeed a happy thought to thus perpetuate in enduring stone the sculptor's admirable conception of the beloved one whose name will always be associated with that of him who sang of her, and to place it in a noble temple in one of the greatest cities of the world, where all may observe with delight that amid the many treasures of genius gathered within its walls, is a silent but eloquent memorial of Scottish purity, love and poetry. In its presence no unhallowed thought can live, and we are transported, as it were, from the surroundings of wealth and busy life, to Scotia's soil and the banks of the Ayr, and into another age, as we realize how akin to all that is best in us to-day was the love of Burns and Mary Campbell. Truly " heart-felt raptures " and " bliss beyond compare " lie deep within pure minds and hearts, awaiting only the touch of Him who wisely made us largely dependent for our happiness upon the love of others.

. . . .

The noblest and the tenderest chapter in the life of Robert Burns is that which tells of his love for Mary Campbell, and it will ever awaken a higher estimate of the hallowed sympathy with which the great Creator binds together the hearts of man and woman. It is filled with the purest radiance, and though death's "untimely frost" fell upon her all too soon, the halo and inspiration of reciprocated love remained with him to the last. His poems addressed to her, ending with the one so inexpressibly sad in its retrospect and prayer, and entitled "To Mary in Heaven," breathe a spirit of pure devotion, and whatever the lights and shadows which enter into other views of him, here is one which all may admire for its undimmed beauty. It is idle to conjecture what might have been the difference to Burns and the world had he wedded his "Sweet Highland Mary," and what it is to love and suffer as did Burns, can be understood only by those who, like him and our brilliant Maryland Poe, who loved Lenore, have loved—and lost. Mary Campbell sleeps in a dingy churchyard at Greenock, but Burns has embalmed her memory in loving verses, and she will be remembered with Dante's Beatrice, and Petrarch's Laura, because true lovers will ever delight to read of the constant love of others, and because it was her most rare fortune to inspire an immortal poet with love for her, and to have him tune his lyre in her praise in verse, which touches millions with its deep and genuine melody and pathos.

HIGHLAND MARY.

By Rev. ARTHUR JOHN LOCKHART.

A SINGLE strain—I turned to see
Who bore that thrilling voice :
Of all the chances to a bard
This was Apollo's choice.

In Love's green lodge I met her first—
The springtide wilderness :
A star come down and changed a maid—
This was her loveliness !

My Una of the Scottish wild—
My Highland Mary—stood
Shedding an angel-light athwart
Her sylvan neighbourhood.

Not buxom-warm like Bonnie Jean,
Yet pearly bright was she ;
She held my heart's keen passion-fire
In awful chastity.

A Grace of shining shapeliness—
Her milk-white feet were bare ;
A glimmering aureole seemed to rest
Upon her golden hair.

One crispèd lock is all I hold,
  To show she once was mine,—
That I have clasped with trembling arms
  A creature so divine.

Pity, and trust, and gentleness
  Were in her soft blue eyes,
That misted with celestial dew,
  Communed of Paradise.

O Sabbath ! sacred more than all
  The holy-gifted span
That light the tearful heritage
  Of toil-encumbered man ;—

That day I never can forget
  When last I met her here :
Sweeter, the singing birds, the bloom
  That decked the opening year.

'Twas in the merrie month of May ;
  The birk-tree's tender green
And cluster'd hawthorns scented flowers
  Along the Ayr were seen.

The laverock darted up on high,
  Scattering his fiery notes ;
And merle and mavis shook the songs
  From their enamoured throats.

And love was in the scented sod,
    And the far-kindled skies ;
And love was in the liquid deeps
    Of Highland Mary's eyes.

Where soft the murmuring waters run
    We roved the lee-lang day :
Blissful the hours ! but swiftly sped
    Each wingèd joy away.

The crystal stream between us twa,—
    We held the Holy Book,
And tossed the dancing drops alight
    From out the singing brook.

We spake the awful name of God,
    We held the Heavens in view,
And swore while earth and skies were fair
    That we would aye be true.

Our happiest hours, our last, were they ;—
    The dusk came stealing on ;
She vanished from my yearning gaze,
    And evermore was gone !

Ah, face of perfect mould ! Ah, eyes,
    That looked so kind on me !
Ah, robber Death ! how could I yield
    My noblest hope to thee !

She is forever with the Spring,
　　Her day is ever fair :
But lonely rings our limpid Faile
　　That runs to meet the Ayr.

Lonely my walk by bank and brae,
　　And 'neath the greenwood tree :
Her grave is in the dinsome town,
　　And near the moaning sea.

But thou, O my leaf-haunting star !
　　Art set within my soul :
Ah, hold thy own wild poet's heart
　　In thy divine control !

If he shall fall, and sorrow sore
　　To feel the wound and stain,
Thy memory, like thy living smile,
　　Shall make him whole again.

When friends and fortune shall disown
　　The erring bard, forlorn,
That thy pure soul forsakes him not
　　Shall mitigate their scorn.

Who dower'd thee with His matchless love
　　Hath filled my fiery heart,
And sent me out among His birds
　　To learn their tuneful art.

I to His mandate have been true ;—
I hear each age prolong
The praise of Scotland's noblest heart,
And Scotland's loftiest song :

For he who loves thee cannot die,—
His lightest word is fame ;
And singing worlds shall weep to hear
His Highland Mary's name.

HIGHLAND MARY.

By THEODORE F. WOLFE, A.M., M.D.

THERE is no stronger proof of the transcending power of the genius of Burns than is found in the fact that, by a bare half dozen of his stanzas, an humble dairy servant—else unheard of outside her parish, and forgotten at her death,— is immortalized as a peeress of Petrarch's Laura and Dante's Beatrice, and has been, for a century, loved and mourned of all the world.

We owe much of our tenderest poesy to the heroines whose charms—oft apparently only to the poets—have attuned the fine fancy and aroused the impassioned muse of enamoured bards ; readers have always exhibited a natural avidity to realize the personality of the beings who inspired the tender lays—prompted often by mere curiosity, but more often by a desire to appreciate the tastes and motives of the poets themselves.   How little is known of Highland Mary, the most famous heroine of modern song, is shown by the brief, incoherent and often contradictory allusions to her which the biographies of the ploughman-poet contain. This paper—prepared during a sojourn in "The Land o' Burns "—while it adds a little to our meagre knowledge of Mary Campbell, aims to present consecutively and congru- ously so much as may now be known of her brief life, her relations to the bard and her sad, heroic death.

She first saw the light, in 1764, at Ardrossan, on the coast of Ayrshire, fifteen miles northward from the " auld town of Ayr."   Her parentage was of the humblest, her

father being a sailor before the mast, and the poor dwelling
which sheltered her was in no way superior to the meanest
of those which we find to-day on the narrow streets of her
village. From her birth-place we see, across the Firth of
Clyde, the beetling mountains of the West Highlands where
she afterward dwelt, and, southward, the great mass of
Ailsa Craig looming, a gigantic pyramid, out of the sea.

Mary was named for her paternal aunt, wife of Peter
M'Pherson, a ship-carpenter of Greenock, in whose house
Mary died. In Mary's infancy her family removed to the
vicinage of Dunoon—on the western shore of the Firth,
eight miles below Greenock—leaving the oldest daughter at
Ardrossan, where she married one Anderson. Mary grew to
young womanhood near Dunoon, then returned to Ayrshire
and found occupation at Coilsfield near Tarbolton, where
her acquaintance with Burns soon began. He once told a
lady of rank that he first saw Mary while walking in the
woods of Coilsfield, and first spoke with her at a rustic merry
making and "having the luck to win her regards from other
suitors," they speedily became intimate. At this period of
life Burns's " eternal propensity to fall in love " was unusually active, even for him, and his passion for Mary (at
this time) was one of several which engaged his heart in the
interval between the reign of Ellison Begbie—the lass of
"twa rogueish een "—and that of " Bonnie Jean." Mary
subsequently became a servant in the house of Burns's land-
lord, Gavin Hamilton, a lawyer of Mauchline, who had early
recognised the genius of the bard and admitted him to an
intimate friendship despite his inferior condition. When
Hamilton was persecuted by the kirk for neglect of its
ordinances, Burns, partly out of sympathy with him, wrote
the satires, " Holy Willie's Prayer," " The Twa Herds,"

and "The Holy Fair," which served to unite the friends more closely, and brought the poet often to the house where Mary was an inmate.

We find this house—a sombre structure of stone, little more pretentious than its neighbours—still standing on the shabby street not far from Armour's cottage, the church of "The Holy Fair," and "Poosie Nansie's" inn, where the "Jolly Beggars" used to congregate. Among the dingy rooms shown us in Hamilton's house is that in which he married Burns to "Bonnie Jean" Armour.

The bard's niece, Miss Begg of Bridgeside, has told the writer that she often heard Burns's mother describe Mary as she saw her at Hamilton's; she had a bonnie face and form, complexion of unusual fairness, soft blue eyes, a profusion of shining hair which fell to her knees, a slender and *petite* figure which made her seem younger than her twenty summers, which won the old lady's heart. This description is, in superlative phrase, corroborated by Lindsay in Hugh Miller's "Recollections:"—she was "beautiful, sylph-like," bust and neck were "exquisitely moulded," her bare arms and feet "had a statue-like symmetry and marble-like whiteness," but it was in her lovely countenance that "nature seemed to have exhausted her utmost skill"— "the loveliest creature I have ever seen," etc. All who have written of her have noticed her sprightly beauty, her good sense, her modesty and self-respect. But these qualities were now insufficient to hold the roving fancy of Burns, whose "susceptibility to immediate impressions" (so-called by Byron, who had the same failing) passes belief. His first ephemeral fancy for Mary took little hold upon his heart, and the best that can be said of it is that it was more innocent than the loves which came before and after it.

Within a stone's throw of Mary dwelt Jean Armour, and
when the former returned to Coilsfield, he promptly fell in
love with Jean and solaced himself with her more buxom
and compliant charms.

It was a year and a half later, when his intercourse with
Jean had burdened him with grief and shame, that the
tender and romantic affection for Mary came into his life.
She was yet at Coilsfield and while he was hiding—his heart
tortured by the apparent perfidy of Jean and all the country-
side condemning his misconduct—his intimacy with Mary
was renewed ; his quickened vision now discerned her
endearing attributes, her trust and sympathy were doubly
precious in his distress, and awoke in him an affection such
as he never felt for any other woman. During a few brief
weeks the lovers spent their evenings and Sabbaths together,
loitering amid the

> Banks and braes and streams around
> The castle o' Montgomery,

talking of the golden days that were to be their's when
present troubles were past ; then came (May 14, 1786) the
parting which the world will never forget, and Mary relin-
quished her service and went to her parents at Campbeltown
—a port of Cantyre behind " Arran's mountain isle." Of
this parting Burns says, in a letter to Thomson ; " we met
by appointment on the second of May in a sequestered spot
on the Ayr, where we spent the day in taking farewell before
she should embark for the West Highlands to prepare
matters among her friends for our projected change of life."
The lovers of Burns linger over this final parting and detail
the impressive ceremonials with which the pair solemnized
their betrothal : they stood on either side of a brook, they

laved their hands in the limpid water and scattered it in the
air to symbolize the purity of their intentions, clasping
hands above on an open Bible they swore to be true to each
other forever, then exchanged Bibles and parted never to
meet more. It is not strange that when death had left him
nothing of her but her poor little Bible, a tress of her golden
hair and a tender memory of her love, the recollection of
this farewell remained in his soul forever. He has pictured
it in the exquisite lines of "Highland Mary" and "To
Mary in Heaven."

In the monument at Alloway—between the "auld haunted
kirk" and the bridge where Maggie lost her tail—we are
shown a memento of the parting ; it is the Bible which
Burns gave to Mary and above which their vows were said.
At Mary's death it passed to her sister, at Ardrossan, who
bequeathed it to her son William Anderson ; subsequently
it was carried to America by one of the family, whence it
has been recovered to be treasured here. It is a poor pocket
edition in two volumes ; within the cover of the first, the
hand of Burns has written : "And ye shall not swear by my
name falsely, I am the Lord." Within the second : "Thou
shalt not forswear thyself but shalt perform unto the Lord
thine oaths." Upon a blank leaf of each volume is impressed Burns's masonic signet, with the signature "Robert
Burns, Mossgiel," written beneath, and to the cover of one
volume is attached a lock of poor Mary's long, bright hair—
her spinning-wheel is preserved in the adjoining cottage.

A visit to the scenes of the brief passion of the pair is a
pleasing incident of our Burns pilgrimage. Coilsfield House
is little changed since Mary dwelt beneath its roof—a great
rambling edifice of gray, weather-worn stone, with a row of
white pillars aligned along its facade, its massive walls em-

bowered in foliage and environed by the grand woods which Burns and Mary knew so well. It was then a seat of Colonel Hugh Montgomerie, Earl of Eglintoune, a patron of Burns, and is now owned by a Mr. Patterson. The name Coilsfield is derived from Coila, the traditional appellation of the surrounding district, now called Kyle. The grounds comprise a billowy expanse of wood and sward ; great reaches of turf, dotted with trees already venerable when the lovers here had their tryst a hundred years ago, slope away from the mansion to the Faile and border its murmuring course to the Ayr. Here we trace with romantic interest the wanderings of the pair during the swift hours of that "last day of parting love," their lingering way 'neath the "wild woods thickening green"—by the pebbled shore of Ayr to the brooklet where their vows were made, and thence along the Faile, to the woodland shades of Coilsfield where—at the close of that winged day—"pledging oft to meet again, they tore themselves asunder." Howitt found at Coilsfield a thorn-tree, called by all the country "Highland Mary's thorn," and believed to be the place of the final parting ; years ago the tree was notched and broken by souvenir seekers—if it be still in existence the present occupant of Coilsfield is unaware."

At the time of his parting with Mary, Burns had already resolved to emigrate to Jamaica, and it has been supposed— from his own statements and those of his biographers—that the pair planned to wed and emigrate together ; but Burns soon abandoned this project and, perhaps, all thought of marrying Mary. The song commencing " Will ye go to the Indies, my Mary ?" has been quoted to show he expected her to accompany him, but he says, in an epistle to Thomson that this was his farewell to her, and in another song—

written while preparing to embark—he declares that it is
leaving Mary that makes him " wish to tarry." Further,
we find that with the first nine pounds received from the
sale of his poems, August, 1786, he purchased a single
passage to Jamaica—manifestly having no intention of
taking her with him.

Her being at Greenock in October, en route to a new place
of service at Glasgow, as some of his biographers have discovered, indicates she had no hope that he would marry
·her, then or soon. True, he afterwards said she came to
Greenock to meet him, but it is certain that he knew
nothing of her being there until after her death. During
the summer of 1786, while she was preparing to wed him,
he indited two love songs to her, but they are not more
glowing than those of the same time to several inamoratas,—
less impassioned than the " Farewell to Eliza " and allusions
to Jean in " Farewell, old Scotia's bleak domains "—and
barely four weeks after his ardent and solemn parting with
Mary we find him writing to Brice : " I do still love Jean
to distraction." Poor Mary ! Possibly the fever mercifully
saved her from dying of a broken heart.

The poet's anomalous affectional condition and conduct
may perhaps be explained by assuming that he loved Mary
as the " creature of a dream," with a refined and spiritual
passion so different from his love for others—and especially
from his conjugal love for Jean—that the passions could
co-exist in his heart. The alternative explanation is that
his love for Mary, while she lived, was by no means the
absorbing passion which he afterwards believed it to have
been. When death had hallowed his memories of her love
and of all their sweet intercourse—beneficent death ! that
beautifies, ennobles, irradiates, in the remembrance of sur-

vivors, the loved ones its touch has taken!—then his soul, swelling with the passion that throbs in the strains of "To Mary in Heaven," would not own to itself that its love had ever been less.

Mary remained at Campbeltown during the summer of 1786. Coming to Greenock in the autumn, she found her brother sick of a malignant fever at the house of her aunt; bravely disregarding danger of contagion, she devoted herself to nursing him, and brought him to a safe convalescence only to be herself stricken by his malady and to rapidly sink and die, a sacrifice to her sisterly affection.

By this time the success of his poems had determined Burns to remain in Scotland, and he returned to Mossgiel, where tidings of Mary's death reached him. His brother relates that, when the letter was handed to him, he went to the window to read it, then his face was observed to change suddenly, and he quickly went out without speaking. In June of the next year he made a solitary journey to the Highlands, apparently drawn by memory of Mary. If, indeed, he dropped a tear upon her neglected grave, and visited her humble Highland home, we may almost forgive him the excesses of that tour—if not the renewed *liaison* with Jean which immediately preceded, and the amorous correspondence with "Clarinda" (Mrs. M'Lehose) which followed it.

Whatever the quality or degree of his passion for Mary living, his grief for her dead was deep and tender, and expired only with his life. Cherished in his heart, it manifested itself now in some passage of a letter—like that to Mrs. Dunlop—now in some pathetic burst of song—like "The Lament" and "Highland Mary"—and again in some emotional act. Of many such acts, narrated to the writer

by Burns's niece, the following is, perhaps, most striking :
The poet attended the wedding of Kirstie Kirkpatrick, a
favourite of his, who often sang his songs for him, and, after
the wedded pair had retired, a lass of the company—
being asked to sing—began " Highland Mary." Its effect
upon Burns " was painful to witness, he started to his feet,
prayed her in God's name to forbear, then hastened to the
door of the marriage chamber and entreated the bride to
come and quiet his mind with a verse or two of ' Bonnie
Doon.' "

But the lines of " To Mary in Heaven " aad the pathetic
incidents of their composition show most touchingly how he
mourned his " fair-haired lassie " years after she ceased to
be.   It was at Ellisland, October 20, 1789, the anniversary
of Mary's death, an occasion which brought afresh to his
heart memories of the tender past : Jean has told us of his
increasing silence and unrest as the day declined, of his
aimless wandering by Nithside at nightfall, of his rapt ab-
straction as he lay pillowed by the sheaves of his stack-yard,
gazing entranced at the " lingering star " above him till the
immortal song was born.

Poor Mary is laid in the burial plot of her uncle in the
west kirkyard of Greenock, near Crawford Street ; our pilgrimage in Burns-land may fitly end at her grave.   A path-
way, beaten by feet of many reverend visitors, leads us to
the spot.

It is so pathetically different from the scenes she loved in
life—the heather-clad slopes of her Highland home, the
seclusion of the wooded braes where she loitered with her
poet-lover.   Scant foliage is about her ; few birds may sing
above her here.   She lies by the wall, narrow streets hem
in the enclosure, the air is sullied by smoke from factories

and from steamers passing within a stone's-throw on the busy Clyde, the clanging of many hammers and the discordant din of machinery and traffic invade the place and sound in our ears as we muse above the ashes of the gentle lassie.

For half a century her grave was unmarked and neglected, then, by subscription, a monument of marble, twelve feet in height, and of graceful proportions, was raised. It bears a sculptural medallion representing Burns and Mary, with clasped hands, plighting their troth. Beneath is the simple inscription, read oft by eyes dim with tears :

ERECTED OVER THE GRAVE OF
HIGHLAND MARY
1842.

" My Mary, dear departed shade,
Where is thy place of blissful rest ? "

REMINISCENCE OF "HIGHLAND MARY."

THE SCENE OF HER DEATH.

From "The Glasgow Herald," January 30th, 1877.

Very little appears to be known of the circumstances connected with the death of Burns's Highland Mary, or of the house in Greenock in which she died. This is accounted for by the fact of Mary Campbell's humble position in life, by that of her relatives, and by the circumstance that the passionate attachment which existed between her and the poet was known only at the time to a few of her immediate relatives. Of course, there is no one living now in Greenock who was contemporary with her uncle or his wife, and the monument erected over her grave in the old West Kirkyard is silent as to the locality of her death. From careful inquiries, however, we are satisfied that the dwelling of her uncle, James Macpherson, was situated at the head of Minch Collop Close, now one of the narrowest and most disreputable parts of Greenock; but being in the immediate neighbourhood of the house in which James Watt, the improver of the steam engine, was born, the locality, at the time of Mary's death, must have been moderately respectable. The dwelling is reached by a dilapidated outside stair, and consists of two small apartments. In connection with Highland Mary's death, the following extract is taken from a letter said to have been written many years ago to a friend by an old shipwright who resided in Greenock. The

letter takes the form of an anecdote told him by another
shipwright, named John Blair, who was a boon companion
of James Macpherson, the uncle of Mary. The writer states
that Blair, one evening in the month of August, 1786, was
taking a walk up the road leading from Greenock to Kilmalcolm, and on reaching the top of Knock-an-air Hill met
Highland Mary. The meeting and subsequent circumstances
attending her death are thus described ;

While I was lookin' at the country, the river, and
Greenock down to the water's edge, and hearkenin' to the
whirr o' the moor fowl as they settled in a black flock on
the farmer's stooks, I sees a braw buxom lass comin' down
the Kilmalcolm-road. She was a weelfaur'd dame, wi'
cheeks like roses. She had on a tartan shawl, an' was car-
rying some things wi' her. I offered to help her to carry
them, which she gladly assented to, for she was tired wi' a
lang journey. She had come frae Ayrshire, and had got a
drive to Kilmalcolm, and was gaun first to Jamie Macpherson, the shipwright's, wha's wife was her cousin, and syne to
Argyle, where her folk belang'd. I kent Jamie as weel's I
ken you, Davie ; we were gude cronies and gude neebours.
Twa or three days after this I chanced to foregather wi'
Jamie. "Man, John," says he to me, "ye're aye speaking
about books an' poetry ; ye'll come doun by the nicht an'
I'll let you see some richt poems." I gaed doun by accord-
ingly, an' got a sicht o' the book he spak o'. It was a
volume of poems by Robert Burns, printed at Kilmarnock.
"It was Mary Campbell, Jean's cousin," Jamie explained,
"wha brought the book wi' her frae Ayr ; it's jist new out,
you see. She's awa to Argyle to see her friends, an' she's
comin' back in a week or twa to be married. And wha do
you think till ?" I said I couldna guess. "Weel, it's jist

to the chiel' wha made that book. She said he had been
fechtin' wi' the ministers, and was thinkin' o' gaun awa to
the West Indies; but she didna care, she was willin' to gang
wi' him." Jamie read a lot o' the poems ower, and we held
at them till twal o'clock. Jamie said he didna a' thegither
like the way the chiel spak o' the kirks, but he thocht "the
lassie might help to haud him straught; and he sudna be
the man to mak' strife amang sweethearts." He let's see a
wee sang the lass had brocht wi' her, beginning—

> " Will ye gang to the Indies, my Mary,
>   An' leave auld Scotland's shore ? "

which Mary had shown as a great secret to his wife, and
which was written upon herself. Mary returned across the
Firth the week after. It was a cold, rainy, muggy day that
she got to the cross, and she had gotten a dreadful chill.
The fever was then ragin' in Greenock, for ye ken wi' our
houses a' huddled thegither, an' the ill water we had then,
an' the foul air that hangs about our narrow wynds and
closes, we never hardly want fever. Puir Mary, onyway,
took it; whether it was the chill she had gotten, or the foul
air of Minch Collop Close, or baith thegither that brocht it
on I canna say, but Mary sickened an' grew worse day by
day. Jamie Macpherson's wife nursed her like a sister ; a
doctor was called in, but naething wad do. Her time was
come. Jamie's wife tell'd me a' about it. She lay in a wee
room aff the kitchen ; there was a chest o' drawers an' a
clock in't, three or four stuffed birds, and a picture of
a naval battle between the French and British, also twa
models of ships. There was a wee window, that neither
opened up nor down ; but the air outside was that
foul wi' vapours that it was maybe better it didna. Nae

doubt, to her comin' out o' the country, the close air that the dwellers' lungs had got used to wad be no beneficial. Man, I whiles think that thae fevers are jist brocht on by the air a'thegither. Whiles the poor sufferer was a wee raivell'd ; whiles she repeated verses out o' the Bible, ane in particular—" Thou shalt not forswear thyself, but shalt perform unto the Lord thine oaths ; " and ance she cried out, " O for a drink o' caller water ! " but it was thocht at that time that water was ill for fevers. But before she died she was quite sensible, an' said to her cousin Jean, " If it had been God's will I wad hae liked to be Robert Burns's wife ; but I ken I'm deein', an' I am quite willin'." " Dinna speak that way, Mary," said Jean, "or ye'll break my heart ; ye'll get better yet, lassie, for a' this." But she did not better ; an' the night following her spirit took its flight from this world of sin and misery, to the great sorrow of all her friends, and, as was kent some years after, to that of her admirer, Robert Burns. Ye ken his sang " Highland Mary " was written about her, and ither sangs o' his, gin I could mind them.

THE MYSTERY OF MARY.

By PETER ROSS.

How or where Robert Burns became acquainted with Mary Campbell is not known, but in all likelihood it was during the time she was employed as a servant in the family of Gavin Hamilton at Mauchline. While Burns was in the midst of his first publication troubles he had another and a still more serious cause for perplexity on his hands. He had courted her who afterwards became his wife, the Bonnie Jean of so many of his finest songs, and she had trusted him too implicitly. Just when his worldly affairs were at their darkest she told him that she was soon to become a mother, and unable to do anything else, he gave her a letter or paper of some sort acknowledging her as his wife—a document which, according to the law of Scotland as commonly understood, made them legally married. When her condition became such that she could no longer hide it from her own family, Jean informed her father and showed him the document. The old man appears to have been insane with anger. He tore the paper into shreds, upbraided his daughter for associating with such a blackguard as Burns, and threatened to clap him into jail. There is no doubt that Burns loved Jean Armour, even although she at first seemed to acquiesce in her father's frantic efforts for vengeance. But when the time was at hand for Jean to become a mother, and when her father was trying to have him arrested, Burns fell head over ears in love with Mary Campbell. One Sunday they met on the banks of the Ayr and solemnly plighted their troth to each other. Mary was sincere in her affection, so was Burns—at least the Bibles which he gave her on the occasion would lead us so to infer. They were inscribed with verses from the Scriptures enforcing fidelity—" And ye shall not swear by My name falsely, I am the Lord," and "Thou shalt not forswear thyself but shalt perform unto the Lord thine oath," while to emphasize his own honesty and unfaltering, he added to his signature his mark as a Royal Arch Mason. They parted at the stream. Mary went to Greenock *en route* to the West Highlands to inform her friends of her approaching marriage to Burns. While sojourning at Greenock, the girl sickened of a fever and died after a brief illness. Such is the story as commonly told by Burns himself and his biographers, but if we examine it, it presents many inconsistencies. By all Burns's editors and biographers, as well as by the poet himself, Mary is represented as a pure, high-minded girl, generous in her impulses, and the very perfection of innocence, and patient—sometimes malicious—investigation has failed to discover the slightest particle of evidence, worthy of the name to prove her to have been in the least degree unworthy of this reputation. Yet, it is impossible to believe otherwise than that she must have known that the morals of Burns were not of the purest, and that she must also have known all about his intimacy with Jean Armour and been fully aware of its result. She must also have learned of Burns's paper acknowledging Jean as his wife, for it was known all over the country. Again, the names and much of the writing on the Bibles given to Mary were afterwards partially obliterated by some one not in the habit of doing work requiring much delicacy of treatment. Now, it seems almost certain that these would not be removed by Mary's

5

friends after her death.   Why should they, since they were
in every way honourable to her ?   Besides, Scotch peasants
never cared to efface anything written or printed which bore
the name of the Deity.   We are left, therefore, to assume
that Mary herself obliterated them, and to believe with Mr.
Scott Douglas that Burns forgot all his vows as soon as she
had passed from his sight, and that on learning this, the
poor creature effaced the names.   Mr. Douglas, who investigated the mystery of Highland Mary with the utmost care
in the hope of unravelling it wrote, "It seems certain that
Burns never whispered her name to a living soul until three
years after her decease.   It was only when the surpassing
beauty and pathos of his sublime dirge 'To Mary in Heaven,'
awakened a curiosity which he could not avoid in some
degree to satisfy, that he uttered a few vague particulars of
her story."   Of Mary's part in the whole transaction, however, we can say nothing.   She died and made no sign, and
amongst all the gossip of the time nothing has survived of
a nature substantial enough to enable us to consider the incident from her point of view.   As to Burns, leaving aside
the mystery with which he has chosen to invest the matter,
and judging him simply by what he has told us and the
events of his life at the time, his conduct was reprehensible
in a marked degree.   This, however, was not the opinion of
Dr. Hately Waddell, one of the poet's most enthusiastic
editors and biographers, and who, as a clergyman, deserves
to have his opinion recorded as a judge of the human con-
science and of the moral law.   He emphatically says, that in
connection with the Highland Mary incident, "there was
neither guilt nor the shadow of guilt on his (Burns's) con-
science."   Still it is evident that Burns, if he remembered
in this love episode anything about Jean Armour, and of

his avowed position as her legal husband (and on this point
there can be no doubt), knew that he had no right to pay
this innocent Highland girl such attentions, that by giving
way to his passion and in binding her love to him, as he did,
with all the superstitious ceremonies so common then
among the simple-minded peasantry, he was weaving a
chain around her which death only could rend asunder.
Judging him by his own record, when Mary went away
from Ayrshire he turned to find other hearts to charm, and
to bask in the sunshine of new smiles. When he learned
of her untimely death, however, he was terribly affected,
and the anniversary of that event, as it came round year
after year, seems never to have been forgotten. He has
immortalized her in some of the most beautiful and affecting lyrics in the entire realm of Scottish poetry, but all the
poetry which has been given to the world since it began will
not compensate for the wanton breaking of one real human
heart.

Such is the story told by Burns and his biographers, and
such are the sentiments to which it gives rise. But there
is a great amount of mystery and discrepancy about it which
has neither been fathomed nor reconciled, and in all proba-
bility never will. It is the only episode in Burns's life
which he did not make perfectly clear to us, and why he
should have so left it we are unable to determine. Probably the best way now to leave it is to say with Dr.
Waddell, that, as a result of her acquaintance with Burns,
Mary has " entered on an immortality more beautiful than
Beatrice's or Laura's, in which respect neither complaint as
against Burns, nor sorrow as for her should be obtruded on
the world. It is enough for Mary and for mankind that
Burns once loved her."

THE COMMON WEIRD.

By *THOMAS C. LATTO,*

Author of "Memorials of Auld Lang Syne," etc., etc.

Why should a simple Ayrshire sang,
    Sae fau'ty in the rhymin',
Gar elders sab an' younkers sigh,
    As gin a knell were chimin'?
There's no a line frae end to end
    But shows a hasty scrievin',
And yet the tones are naething else
    But an immortal grievin'.

'Tis but a ploughman laddie's moan,
    Micht hae been pour'd by ony;
Her manners micht na gentry been,—
    Maybe she was na bonny;
But the brief lines were floatit far,—
    Fame to the skies upbore them;
Men melted at the thrillin' air,
    While Beauty quaver'd o'er them.

Its magic darts to a' the airts
    Where flocketh human nature;
A' croon it, even at the Poles,
    An' doun to the Equator;

It calms the burst o' hopeless wae,
 It saftens tears when rollin' ;
It soothes, tho' little it may help ;—
 There's mickle in consolin'.

Tho' in the dirge there breathes a wail,
 O' manly sense it savours,
An' sae to thousands it appeals
 Wha laugh at poet's havers :
Altho' her rank a servan' lass,
 Thrang tentin' o' her dairy,
What miracles are brought to pass
 Thro' this bit lilt o' Mary.

There's hardly ane whase flow'r o' love
 Has not untimely wilted,
There's scarce a lad e'er gaed to woo
 But was beguil'd or jilted ;
Or if he won a lassie dear
 To cuddle in his bosie,
He had to grieve o'er graces fled—
 Pale lips that ance were rosy.

Cauld critics puzzle at the power,
 But daur na sneer nor brand it ;
It takes a heart to read it wi',
 They canna understand it.
Why should this feelin' spread sae wide,
 And never seem to vary ?
Because 'tis felt by ane an' a'
 HE lost a " Hielant Mary."

DR. ROBERT CHAMBERS' VIEWS.

AS RECORDED IN HIS 1851-3 EDITION OF BURNS.

. . . . MARY CAMPBELL was of Highland parentage, from the neighbourhood of Dunoon, on the Firth of Clyde. Her father was a sailor in a revenue cutter, the station of which being at Campbelton in Kintyre, his family now resides there. We may presume that the young woman was somewhat superior in cast of mind, manners and intelligence to her situation, as it is ascertained that she had spent some of her youthful years in the family of the Rev. David Campbell of Loch Ranza, in Arran, a relation of her mother. She had afterwards been induced by another relation, a Mrs. Isabella Campbell, who was housekeeper to a family in Ayrshire, to come to that county and take a situation as a servant. There is some obscurity about the situations and movements of Mary ; but the surviving children of Mrs. Hamilton are probably right in thinking that she was nursemaid to their deceased brother Alexander, who was born in July 1785, and that she saw him through some of the early stages of infancy before leaving their house. As a stranger serving only for a short time in the village, she has been little remembered there. Mrs. Begg recollects no sort of reference to her at Mossgiel, except from the poet himself, when he told John Blane one day that " Mary had refused to meet him in the old Castle,"—the dismantled tower of the priory, near Hamilton's house.

Thrown off and heart-wrung as he now was by Jean, it is natural enough that he should revert to Mary Campbell. On the eve of a voyage to the West Indies, in a humble capacity, it was not desirable that he should unite himself with any woman, however dear ; but his soul rushed to a compensation for the desertion of Armour—prudential considerations, as usual with him where affairs of the heart were concerned, formed little or no impediment—he betook himself to Mary, and found her willing to be his for life, notwithstanding all that had passed with Jean. Such at least is the view we take of the circumstances, from all that has transpired. It was agreed that Mary should give up her place and go home for a short time to her friends in the Highlands, in order to arrange matters for her union with the poet. But before going—on the second Sunday of May, the 14th of the month, being the day before the term at which servants commence and complete engagements in Scotland—Mary and Burns had a farewell meeting in a sequestered spot on the banks of the Ayr. The day and the place are indicated by himself. It is probable that the lovers did not confine themselves to the banks of the Ayr, but digressed into the minor Valley of the Faile, where the woods of Coilsfield compose many beautiful scenes. . . . The date of Burns's attachment to Highland Mary, and several of the circumstances connected with it, have been matter of doubt and obscurity till lately. In January, 1850, Mr. William Douglas, engraver, Edinburgh, brought before the Society of Scottish Antiquaries an elaborate paper, making it all but perfectly certain that the affair was, what had never been hitherto suspected, an episode in the attachment to Jean Armour. He showed that it could not have been, as several biographers had surmised, a strictly juvenile

attachment, as the Bible is dated in 1782, and the name of
the poet is followed by the word "Mossgiel," a place with
which he had no connection till Martinmas 1783, when he
was nearly 25 years of age, and where he did not reside till
March of the ensuing year.   He also traced the connection
between this attachment and the design of going to the
West Indies, a design of which we hear at no earlier period
of his life than spring 1786.   This connection appears
strongly in a song (The Highland Lassie) which Burns afterwards published in "Johnson's Scots Musical Museum."
Burns himself, in the notes on "Johnson's Museum,"
which he wrote for Captain Riddel, says regarding this
song, "it was a composition of mine in very early life, before I was at all known in the world.   My Highland lassie
was a warm-hearted, charming young creature as ever
blessed a man with generous love."   And then he goes on to
relate the story of their parting.   Now the whole circumstances detailed in this little ballad—his love, his desire of
fortune for the sake of the loved one, and especially his
being compelled by the frowns of fortune to cross the raging
sea—entirely answer to the crisis at which Burns had now
arrived, and they do not at all answer to any other period of
his life of which we have any knowledge.   There is another
song, which was found amongst the poet's manuscripts after
his death, and which answers perfectly to the circumstances
and feelings which have been represented.   It is entitled by
himself "A Prayer for Mary."   Burns also told Mr. Thomson, in 1792, "In my very early years, when I was thinking
of going to the West Indies, I took the following farewell of
a dear girl, (Will ye go to the Indies, my Mary?)   But for
the phrases, "very early life," and "my very early years,"
there could be no difficulty in assigning "My Highland

Lassie," and " Will ye go to the Indies, my Mary ? " which is evidently another expression of the same passion, to the date 1786 ; but Mr. Douglas argued, that either Burns felt as if the lapse of six years had brought him out of youth into middle age, or he wished to maintain a mystery regarding the story of Mary. For his studying to keep the matter in some obscurity there certainly might be motives of some cogency ; for one, a dislike to recall before the mind of his wife an affair which had come somewhat awkwardly between them, and run nigh to sever them for ever. But then it may be said, Burns was a man above disguises and secrets. So he was in general ; yet did he not say in a poem which left his hand this very month :—

> —— " Aye keep something to yoursel'
> Ye scarcely tell to ony."

The ingenuity and industry of Mr. Douglas had so nearly succeeded in solving this curious problem in Burns's history, that it is almost a pity to add to the evidence he has brought forward. So it is, however, that, as will be seen hereafter, proofs of a more satisfactory kind for the same conclusion have been discovered.

.   .   .   .

Mary, we are to presume from the narrative of the poet, had proceeded, immediately after this parting, to Campbeltown, where her parents then resided. She had spent the summer there ; but there is no evidence that she had taken any steps in arranging matters for a union with Burns, although it is believed that she received letters from him. After having spent the summer at home, she agreed, at the recommendation of her former patroness, Mrs. Isabella Campbell, to accept a new situation for the term beginning at Martin-

mas, in the family of Colonel M'Ivor, in Glasgow. A cousin
of Mary's mother was the wife of one Peter Macpherson, a
ship carpenter at Greenock. It being determined that her
younger brother Robert should be entered as an apprentice,
her father came to Greenock to make the proper arrangements, and Mary accompanied him, professedly on her way
to Glasgow for the purpose of entering on her service with
Col. M'Ivor, but secretly perhaps with the further design
of taking a final farewell to Burns when he should depart
for the West Indies ; for Burns has expressly said that she
crossed the Sea (the Firth of Clyde) to meet him. There
was what is called a *brothering feast* at Macpherson's on
Robert Campbell being admitted to the craft, and Mary
gave her assistance in serving the company. Next morning,
the boy Robert was so indisposed as to be unable to go to
his work. When Macpherson came home to breakfast, he
asked what had detained him from the yard, and was told
that the young man was very poorly. Mary jocularly observed that he had probably taken a little too much after
supper last night, and Macpherson to keep up the badinage
said, "Oh, then, it is just as well, in case of the worst, that
I have agreed to purchase that lair in the kirk-yard," referring to a place of sepulture which he had just secured for
his family—a very important matter in Greenock, as there
was then no resting-place for the remains of those who did
not possess such property, except the·corner assigned to
strangers and paupers, or a grave obtained by favour from
a friend. The young man's illness proved more serious than
was at first supposed, and Mary attended him with great
tenderness and assiduity. In a few days Robert began to
recover, but at the same time Mary drooped, and became
seriously unwell. Her friends believed that she suffered

from the cast of an evil eye, and recommended her father
to go to a cross burn—that is, a place where two burns
meet—and select seven smooth stones from the channel,
boil them with new milk for a certain time, and then give
her the milk to drink. It must be remembered that these
were Highland people, and that the Highlanders are to this
day full of superstitious notions. The drink was duly prepared as had been recommended, and given to Mary ; but
her illness was soon declared to be of a malignant species
then prevalent in the town, and in a few days the poor girl
died. She was buried in the *lair* which her relative had so
recently bought, being the first of the family who was placed
in it. Such are the particulars derived from Macpherson's
daughter, and from a male relative of the family (Mr. J. C.
Douglas, clothier, Greenock), who has often conversed on
the subject with Mary's mother. There seems to be no
good reason for doubting them, or any of them. The only
point in which the story is defective is the date, a matter
regarding which the memory is apt to be less faithful than
with respect to events. There is, unluckily, no register of
deaths or funerals for this period in Greenock. In my
efforts, by other means, to ascertain the date of Mary's
death, I met for some time with little success. On a visit
to the town for the purpose of making investigations, my
first attention was given to Mary's grave. It is in the
burial-ground of the West Church, the original and principal parish of Greenock—a melancholy and half-deserted
precinct, so close to the Firth of Clyde, that a stone could
be thrown into it from the passing steamers. In a central
situation are two flat stones, recording the ancestors of the
illustrious James Watt. Near the west end is the little
plot which had belonged to Peter Macpherson, the ship

carpenter. Shading it from the setting sun is a tall structure which a few admirers of Burns have erected for the
commemoration of her whom the poet loved. It contains a
sculpture representing the parting of the lovers, surmounted
by a figure weeping over an urn, on which is inscribed the
name MARY. At the foot of this lofty structure nestles the
original *head stone* of Macpherson. In its semi-lunar upper
compartment are carved the tools of a carpenter, with the
date 1760. Underneath, on the square body of the stone,
is the legend—" This place belongs to Peter Macpherson,
ship-carpenter, in Greenock, and Mary Campbell his spouse,
and their children, 1787." There was an uncertainty here.
The stone might have been erected in 1760 by some member
of Macpherson's family, from whom he had inherited it ;
and notwithstanding the legend and second date, Mary
might have been buried there at any time from 1760 down-
ward. I observed, however, that the legend and second
date are inscribed upon a surface half an inch or so inward
from that on which the tools were carved, as if an earlier
inscription had been obliterated—implying that the stone
had undergone a renovation in 1787. If that was to be re-
garded as a doing of Macpherson when he became possessed
of the *lair*, the tendency of the evidence might be said to
be in favour of a late, rather than an early date for the
death of Mary. Still the matter was left at an unsatisfac-
tory point. At this stage of the enquiry it was brought to
mind that there was a Register of Lairs, in which it might
be hoped that the date of Macpherson's purchase was entered. A wretched tattered old volume was found buried
in a mass of similar rubbish in the possession of Mr. Teulon,
Superintendent of the burying grounds of Greenock, by

whose obliging assistance, with no small difficulty, an entry was at length found, to the following effect :—

> " 1760.   feet
> Jany. 14. Duncan Robertson, Carpenter 6 £0 9 0
> 1786.
> Oct. 12.   This lair is this day transferred to Peter Macpherson, ship-carpenter in Greenock."

There could not of course remain the slightest doubt that the ground which contains the ashes of Highland Mary was bought by her relative at the very time when Robert Burns designed to sail from Greenock for the West Indies. Macpherson had, exactly as I conjectured, succeeded to a stone, which he had renovated, preserving only the sculpture of his predecessor's emblem of trade, because these were equally suitable for himself. Unless, then, we are to reject the family story entirely, and suppose it possible that Mary was buried here while Duncan Robertson possessed the ground, which, I am informed, the customs of sculpture in Greenock render to the last degree improbable, we must admit that her death took place in the latter part of 1786— consequently after her poet-lover had broken off his match with Jean Armour—in short, the piteous tale of the Highland Lassie comes in as one of several episodes that chequered the main attachment of Burns's life, and which terminated in making him at length a husband.

TO BURNS'S "HIGHLAND MARY."

From "Blackwood's Magazine," v. lxvii., 1850, p. 309.

I.

O loved by him whom Scotland loves,
　Long loved, and honoured duly
By all who love the bard who sang
　So sweetly and so truly !
In cultured dales his song prevails,
　Thrills o'er the eagles aëry—
Ah ! who that strain has caught, nor sighed
　For Burns's " Highland Mary ? "

II.

I wandered on from hill to hill,
　I fear'd nor wind nor weather ;
For Burns beside me trod the moor,—
　Beside me pressed the heather.
I read his verse—his life—alas !
　O'er that dark shades extended :—
With thee at last, and him in thee,
　My thoughts their wanderings ended.

III.

His golden hours of youth were thine—
Those hours whose flight is fleetest ;
Of all his songs to thee he gave
The greatest and the sweetest.
Ere ripe the fruit, one branch he brake,
All rich with bloom and blossom ;
And shook its dews, its incense shook,
Above thy brow and bosom.

IV.

And when his Spring, alas, how soon !
Had been by care subverted,
His Summer, like a god repulsed,
Had from his gates departed ;
Beneath the evening star once more,
Star of his morn and even !
To thee his suppliant hands he spread,
And hail'd his love " in heaven."

V.

And if his spirit in a waste
Of shame too oft was squandered,
And if too oft his feet ill-starred
In ways erroneous wandered :
Yet still his spirit's spirit bathed
In purity eternal ;
And all fair things thro' thee retained
For him their aspect vernal.

VI.

Nor less than tenderness remained
.   Thy favouring love implanted ;
Compunctious pity, yearnings vague
    For love to earth not granted ;
Preserve with freedom, female grace
    Well matched with manly vigour,
In songs where fancy twined her wreaths
    Round judgment's stalwart rigour.

VII.

A mute but strong appeal was made ·
    To him by feeblest creatures ;
In his large heart each had a part—
    That part had found in Nature's.
The wildered sheep, sagacious dog,
    Old horse reduced and crazy,
The field-mouse by the plough upturned,
    And violated daisy.

VIII.

In him there burned that passionate glow,
    All Nature's soul and savour,
Which gives its hue to every flower,
    To every fruit its flavour.
Nor less the kindred power he felt,
    That love of all things human,
Whereof the fiery centre is
    The love man bears to woman.

IX.

He sang the dignity of man,
 Sang woman's grace and goodness ;
Passed by the world's half-truths, her lies
 Pierced through with lance-like shrewdness.
Upon life's broad highways he stood,
 And aped nor Greek nor Roman ;
But snatched from heaven Promethean fire
 To glorify things common.

X.

He sang of youth, he sang of age,
 Their joys, their griefs, their labours ;
Felt with, not for, the people ; hailed
 All Scotland's sons his neighbours :
And therefore all repeat his verse—
 Hot youth or graybeard, steady,
The boatman on Loch Etive's waves,
 The shepherd on Ben Ledi.

XI.

He sang from love of song : his name
 Dunedin's cliff resounded :—
He left her faithful to a fame
 On truth and nature founded.
He sought true fame not loud acclaim ;
 Himself and Time he trusted :
For laurels crackling in the flame
 His fine ear never lusted.

6

XII.

He loved, and reason had to love
  The illustrious land that bore him :
Where'er he went like heaven's broad tent
  A star-bright Past hung o'er him.
Each isle had fenced a saint recluse,
  Each tower a dying hero ;
Down every mountain gorge had rolled
  The flood of foemen flying.

XIII.

From age to age that land had paid
  No alien throne submission,
For feudal faith had been her law,
  And freedom her tradition.
Where frowned the rocks had Freedom smiled,
  Snug 'mid the shrill wind's whistle,
So England prized her garden Rose,
  But Scotland loved her Thistle !

XIV.

The land thus pure from foreign foot,
  Her growing powers thus centered
Around her heart, with other lands
  The race historic entered.
Her struggling dawn, convulsed or bright,
  Worked on thro' storms and troubles,
Whilst a heroic line of kings
  Strove with heroic nobles.

XV.

Fair field alone the brave demand,
  And Scotland ne'er had lost it :
And honest prove the hate and love
  To objects meet adjusted.
Intelligible course was hers,
  By safety tried or danger :
The native was for native known,
  The stranger known for stranger.

XVI.

Honour in her a sphere had found,
  Nobility a station,
The patriot's thought the last it sought,
  And virtue—toleration.
Her will and way had ne'er been crossed
  In fatal contradiction ;
Nor loyalty to treason soured,
  Nor faith abused with fiction.

XVII.

Can song be mute where hearts are sound ?
  Weak doubts—away we fling them !
The land that breeds great men, great deeds,
  Should ne'er lack bards to sing them.
That rigour, sense, and mutual truth
  Which baffled each invader,
Shall fill her marts, and feed her arts,
  While peaceful olives shade her.

XVIII.

Honour to Scotland and to BURNS !
 In him she stands collected.
A thousand streams one river make,
 Thus genius, heaven-directed,
Conjoins all separate veins of power
 In one great soul creation,
And blends a million men to make
 The Poet of the nation !

XIX.

Honour to BURNS ? and her who first
 Let loose the abounding river
Of music from the Poet's heart,
 Borne through all lands for ever !
How much to her mankind has owed
 Of song's selected treasures !
Unsweetened by her kiss, his lips
 Had sung for other measures.

XX.

Be green for aye, green bank and brae
 Around Montgomery's Castle !
Blow there ye earliest flowers ! and there
 Ye sweetest song birds nestle !
For there was ta'en that last farewell,
 In hope, indulged how blindly ;
And there was given that long last gaze
 " That dwelt " on him " sae kindly."

XXI.

No word of thine recorded stands,
  Few words that hour were spoken :
Two Bibles there were interchanged
  And some slight love-gift broken.
And there thy cold, faint hands he pressed,
  Thy head by dewdrops misted ;
And kisses, ill-resisted first,
  At last were unresisted.

XXII.

Ah, cease !—she died.   He too is dead.
  Of all her girlish graces,
Perhaps one nameless lock remains :
  The rest stern Time effaces.
Dust lost in dust.   Not so ; a bloom
  Is hers which ne'er can wither ;
And in that lay, which lives for aye,
  The twain live on together.

HIGHLAND MARY'S GRAVE.

FROM " THE PEOPLE'S JOURNAL."

DURING the past few years the Greenock Burns Club has caused the grave of Highland Mary to be dressed and planted with flowers. But the ground at one time having sunk below the level of the adjoining graves, it was too wet for successful growth, and even when leaves did appear, they were not allowed to remain more than a few days till they were plucked and carried away as mementoes. On one occasion, two gentlemen from a distance visited the grave, and expressed astonishment that it was not planted with flowers. The reason was explained to them, whereupon one walked away a few feet, plucked a flower, which he threw on Highland Mary's grave, and then asked his friend to lift it and put it in his pocket-book, because they would be able to say when they got home that it was from Highland Mary's grave. The Committee of the Club lately (1891) resolved to take the advice of a practical gardener as to the best mode of decorating the grave, and asked Mr. Hugh Crichton, chief gardener to Mrs. J. T. Caird, Belleaire, to report. That gentleman stated that the ground from its situation was unsuitable for growing plants or flowers, and recommended that the hollow of the ground should be filled up with cement, and that white boulders should be broken up and placed in the cement, the grave thus being arched over. That suggestion has been carried out, and has a very pleasing appearance. The Committee of the Club got the monument

scraped and repainted. The old headstone, which had sunk
into the ground so that only part of the lettering could be
read, was raised and built on a new foundation. This stone
has been cleaned and repainted, and it is just in front of
Highland Mary's monument. The following is the inscription on the old stone :—

This Burying Place
Belongs to PETER M'PHERSON,
Ship Carpenter, Greenock,
and MARY CAMPBELL,
His Spouse, and
Their Children.

1787.

Where this inscription is cut the stone is at least a quarter
of an inch thinner than the top piece. This is evidence that
the name of the first purchaser of the ground had been hewn
off. On the thick part of the stone are the carpenters'
insignia—a mallet, compass, caulking-iron, etc. As the first
purchaser and M'Pherson were both ship carpenters, the
coat-of-arms had been allowed to remain. The railings have
been repainted, the tops tipped with gold. There is a wire-
netting inside the railing to prevent persons from attempting
to remove the broken stones that are set in the cement. As
it was well known that Highland Mary was the first that
was interred in the ground, and that her uncle only purchased it a few months before Mary's death, it was often a
cause of astonishment what the figures 1760 on the upper
part of the stone meant. On referring to the Lair Holders'
Book, we found the following entry :—" January 14th, 1760.
—Purchased by Duncan Robertson, carpenter, six feet for
9s." On October 12, 1780, there is an entry showing that
the ground was purchased by Peter M'Pherson, Highland

Mary's uncle, from Robertson. There is also evidence that the stone has borne a different inscription from what it now does, and it is supposed that while it was in Robertson's possession the lettering was his, but when purchased by Peter M'Pherson the lettering had been hewn out. The very tasteful manner in which the grave has been dressed and decorated reflects credit on the Club and also the community. The grave immediately to the north of Highland Mary's belongs to Mr. Colin Rae-Brown, now of London. He is a great admirer of Burns, and was the moving spirit in getting up the Burns centenary in 1859, and was Secretary of the Glasgow Committee. He designed the medal that was worn that night in commemoration of Burns, and a few years ago presented a medal and the original die to the Greenock Club.

HIGHLAND MARY.

By *JOHN H. INGRAM.*

THE most romantic episode in the chequered career of the Ayrshire bard is that connected with Mary Campbell, the heroine of several of his most impassioned lyrics. Many of Burns's biographers have exercised their ingenuity in endeavours to either clear up or further mystify the facts of this interesting interlude in his life. Dr. Currie, in his attempt to render his history of the poet acceptable to his surviving relatives, readily availed himself of Burns's own words, and placed the "Highland Mary" epoch in the "very early years" of his hero's career. Lockhart, unable or unwilling to contradict his predecessor, did his best to confirm his story. Succeeding biographers either followed blindly in the footsteps of their forerunners, or arrived at the comforting conclusion that "Highland Mary" was a myth—nothing more than a poetic fiction.

The discovery in 1840 of the two-volumed Bible mentioned by Cromek, in his account of the plighted troth on the banks of Ayr, re-opened the whole question of the "Highland Mary" episode, and caused its incidents to be investigated anew. Mr. W. Scott Douglas took the affair in hand, and after much research arrived at the doubtless correct conclusion that the solemn betrothal and final parting of Burns and Mary, instead of having happened in the poet's earlier years, must have taken place in 1786, just at that terrible period in his life when, half-maddened by the treatment he was receiving from Jean Armour and her father, he determined to emigrate to the West Indies.

Mary Campbell, daughter of a sailor from the vicinity of
Dunoon, was a nursemaid in the household of Gavin Hamilton, that friend of Burns of whom so much is heard in the
poet's history.   In his edition of 1851, Chambers says of
Mary Campbell, that it may be assumed " the young
woman was somewhat superior in cast of mind, manners,
and intelligence in her situation, as it is ascertained that she
had spent some of her youthful years in the family of the
Rev. David Campbell, of Loch Ranza, in Arran, a relation
of her mother."

Burns, it will be seen, refers to Mary, to " my Highland
Lassie," as " a warm-hearted, charming young creature as
ever blessed a man with a generous love," and in another
letter says, " When I was thinking of going to the West
Indies I took this farewell—' Will ye go to the Indies, my
Mary ? '—of a dear girl."

The parting of Burns and Mary on the banks of the Ayr
must have taken place on the 14th May, 1786, and her
death at Greenock on or about the 20th October following.
The enduring nature of the poet's affection for Mary Campbell is proved, not only by various circumstances in his life
and passages in his letters, but notably by the fact that his
memorial verses to " My Mary, dear departed shade," were
not composed until three years after her death, and his
latter tribute to " Highland Mary" was not produced until
the 14th November, 1792, six years later ; proofs of his
fidelity to his promise to her in the lines :—

> " She has my heart, she has my hand,
>   By sweet truth (troth ?) and honour's band,
>   Till the mortal stroke shall lay me low,
>   I'm thine, my Highland lassie, O ! "

In 1842 a handsome monument was erected upon the place of Mary's interment in the West Churchyard, Greenock. The history of the two-volumed Bible already referred to is quite romantic. The Bible, we are informed, was found in the possession of a family in Montreal, Canada. The owners, relatives apparently of Mary Campbell, to whose surviving sister at Ardrossan the Bible came, being in straitened circumstances, were anxious to dispose of the valuable heirloom. The manner in which this memento of the bard came into the hands of the family having been satisfactorily explained, a certain number of Scotchmen in Montreal purchased it for transmission to their native land. Mr. Robert Weir, junior, of Montreal, in a letter to his father at Glasgow, said, "By the *Mohawk,* I will send to your care the identical Bibles presented by Burns to his Highland Mary, along with a lock of her hair, to be by you safely transmitted to the Provost of Ayr, for the purpose of being deposited in Burns's monument, on the banks of the bonnie Doon."

This offering to the fatherland from her far-away children has been safely placed in the proposed resting place at Alloway. The Bible, which is only 24mo in size, was printed in 1782, by the "assigns of Alexander Kincaid." The two volumes, upon their receipt at Alloway, were found to be in a good state of preservation, although much worn. They were originally plainly bound in calf and gilt. On the first leaf of the first volume was written, in the handwriting of Burns, "And ye shall not swear by my name falsely—I am the Lord. Levit., 16th chap., 12th verse." On the opposite leaf was drawn the mason mark of secrecy, and a name inscribed, but it has become so worn that it is difficult to say whether it is intended for "Robert Burns" or "Mary

Campbell." The whole page has been crumpled and torn, either purposely or by much fingering. The blank leaf at the end of the volume contained an affecting relic, that is to say, an unusually long lock of auburn hair from the head of Highland Mary. The lock was affixed to the leaf by a tiny pin, and two little pieces of paper wafered over it. This hair is religiously guarded, together with the Bible, in the mausoleum at Alloway. The front leaf of the second volume is inscribed, "Thou shalt not forswear thyself, but shalt perform unto the Lord thine oaths. Matt., 5th ch., 33rd verse." On the opposite page, although somewhat mutilated, is distinctly, in the poet's own handwriting, "Robert Burns, Mossgiel."

Thus Cromek's story has been confirmed, and some of Burns's most impassioned lyrics explained, as far as explanation was needed, by the recovery of this Bible on the other side of the Atlantic ! Long may this relic rest undisturbed in its present sanctuary !

HIGHLAND MARY.

FROM THE "LIFE AND LAND OF BURNS."

By *ALLAN CUNNINGHAM.*

IT is the privilege of genius to confer immortality on things mortal, and give to beauty a fame which can die only with the language in which that fame is bestowed. All the true songs of our nation have been written from the heart, and addressed not to creatures of fancy, but to beings of flesh and blood-warm and real. This is known to the world, who have shown at all times a lively curiosity to learn the history of those who have given life to poetry, and to whose charms we are indebted for the finest productions of the muse. Who would be unwilling to hear the story of the Rosalind of Spenser, the Sacharissa of Waller, or the Highland Mary of Robert Burns ?

Mary Campbell, for such is the name of the most famous of the heroines of northern song, was a mariner's daughter, a native of Ardrossan, in Ayrshire ; and lived, when she won the heart of the poet, in the humble situation of dairymaid in the "Castle of Montgomery." All who have written of her, have spoken of her beauty, the swarm of admirers which her loveliness brought, and the warmth, yet innocence, of her affection for the poet of her native hills. A single song is all that the prolific muse of Burns addressed to her before "hungry ruin had him in the wind ; " and he was about to quit the banks of the Ayr, of the Irvine, and

of the Doon, for the burning shores of the West Indies.   It
was then that he addressed to her the farewell song :—

> " Will ye go to the Indies, my Mary,
>   And leave auld Scotia's shore ?
> Will ye go to the Indies, my Mary,
>   Across th' Atlantic's roar ? "

And it would seem that she had accepted the poet as her
husband, and was preparing to depart for the land of the
lime and the orange, when the hand of death was upon her.
But all this has been told by the poet himself.   " After a
pretty long trial," says Burns, " of the most ardent reciprocal affection, we met, by appointment, on the second
Sunday of May, in a sequestered spot on the banks of the
Ayr, where we spent a day in taking a farewell, before she
should embark for the West Highlands, to arrange matters
among her friends for our projected change of life.   At the
close of the autumn following, she crossed the sea to meet
me at Greenock, where she had scarce landed when she was
seized with a malignant fever, which hurried my dear girl
to her grave in a few days, before I could even learn of her
illness."   The poet has pictured those touching moments in
verse :—

> " How sweetly bloom'd the gay green birk,
>   How rich the hawthorn's blossom,
> As underneath their fragrant shade,
>   I clasp'd her to my bosom !
> The golden hours, on angel wings,
>   Flew o'er me and my dearie ;
> For dear to me, as light and life,
>   Was my sweet Highland Mary."

Another hand has added to the picture. " This adieu
was performed," says Cromek, "in a striking and moving
way ; the lovers stood on each side of a small brook, they
laid their hands in the stream, and holding a Bible between
them, pronounced their vows to be faithful to each other.
They parted, never to meet again." The spot where this
farewell took place is still pointed out.

The Bible on which they plighted their faith was long in
the possession of the sister of Mary Campbell. On the first
volume is written by the hand of Burns : " And ye shall
not swear by my name falsely : I am the Lord." Leviticus,
chap. xix., verse 12. On the second volume, the same hand
has written : "Thou shalt not forswear thyself, but shalt
perform unto the Lord thine oaths." St. Matthew, chap. v.,
verse 33. And on the blank leaves of both volumes is impressed his mark as a mason, and also signed below,
" Robert Burns, Mossgiel."

Burns's affection for the early object of his love died only
with him. More than three years after the death of Mary
Campbell, " whose bosom," to use his own language, " was
fraught with truth, honour, constancy, and love," he wrote
one of the most exquisite of his poems—the address " To
Mary in Heaven." Sweetly and well has Campbell sung in
his Ode to the Memory of Burns :—

> " Who that has melted o'er his lay,
>   To Mary's soul in Heaven above,
>   But pictur'd sees, in fancy strong,
>   The landscape and the live-long day,
>   That smil'd upon their mutual love ?
>   Who that has felt, forgets the song ? "

HIGHLAND MARY.

FROM " LOVES OF THE POETS."

By MRS. JAMIESON.

WHILE my thoughts are yet with Burns,—his name before
me,—my heart and my memory still under that spell of
power which his genius flings around him, I will add a few
words on the subject of his supernumerary loves ; for he has
celebrated few imaginary heroines. Of these rustic divinities,
one of the earliest, and by far the most interesting was Mary
Campbell, (his " Highland Mary,") the object of the deepest
passion Burns ever felt ; the subject of some of his loveliest
songs, and of the elegy " To Mary in Heaven."

Whatever this young girl may have been in person or condition, she must have possessed some striking qualities and
charms to have inspired a passion so ardent, and regrets so
lasting, in a man of Burns's character. She was not his
first love, nor his second, nor his third ; for from the age of
sixteen, there seems to have been no interregnum in his
fancy. His heart, he says, was " completely tender, and
eternally lighted up by some goddess or other." His
acquaintance with Mary Campbell began when he was
about two or three-and-twenty ; he was then residing at
Mossgiel, with his brother, and she was a servant on a
neighbouring farm. Their affection was reciprocal, and they
were solemnly plighted to each other. " We met," says
Burns, " by appointment, on the second Sunday in May, in
a sequestered spot by the banks of the Ayr, where we spent

a day in taking a farewell, before she should embark for the West Highlands, to arrange matters among her friends for our projected change of life." " This adieu," says Mr. Cromek, " was performed with all those simple and striking ceremonials which rustic sentiment has devised to prolong tender emotions and to impose awe. The lovers stood on each side of a small purling brook ; they laved their hands in the stream, and holding a Bible between them, pronounced their vows to be faithful to each other." This very Bible has recently been discovered in the possession of Mary Campbell's sister. On the boards of the old Testament is inscribed in Burns's hand-writing, "And ye shall not swear by my name falsely, I am the Lord."—Levit., chap. xix., v. 12. On the boards of the New Testament, "Thou shalt not forswear thyself, but shalt perform unto the Lord thine oaths."—Matt., chap. v., v. 33, and his own name in both. Soon afterwards, disasters came upon him, and he thought of going to try his fortune in Jamaica. Then it was, that he wrote the simple, wild, but powerful lyric, " Will ye go to the Indies, my Mary ? "

As I have seen among the Alps the living streams rise, swelling and bubbling, from some cleft in the mountain's breast, then, with a broken and troubled impetuosity, rushing amain over all impediments,—then leaping, at a bound, into the abyss below ; so this song seems poured forth out of the full heart, as if a gush of passion had broken forth, that could not be restrained ; and so the feeling seems to swell and hurry through the lines, till it ends in one wild burst of energy and pathos—

> " And curst be the cause that shall part us—
> The hour, and the moment of time ! "

7

A few months after this "day of parting love," on the banks of the Ayr, Mary Campbell set off from Inveraray to meet her lover, as I suppose, to take leave of him, for it should seem that no thoughts of a union could then be indulged. Having reached Greenock, she was seized with a malignant fever, which hurried her to the grave in a few days ; so that the tidings of her death reached her lover, before he could even hear of her illness. How deep and terrible was the shock to his strong and ardent mind,—how lasting the memory of his early love, is well known. Years after her death, he wrote the song of "Highland Mary."

The elegy, "To Mary in Heaven," was written about a year after his marriage, on the anniversary of the day on which he heard of the death of Mary Campbell. The account of the feelings and the circumstances under which it was composed, was taken from the recital of Bonnie Jean herself, and cannot be read without a thrill of emotion. "According to her, Burns had spent that day, though labouring under a cold, in the usual work of his harvest, and apparently in excellent spirits. But as the twilight deepened, he appeared to grow 'very sad about something,' and at length wandered out into the barn-yard, to which his wife, in her anxiety for his health, followed him, entreating him, in vain, to observe that frost had set in, and to return to his fire-side. On being again and again requested to do so, he always promised compliance, but still remained where he was, striding up and down slowly, and contemplating the sky, which was singularly clear and starry. At last, Mrs. Burns found him stretched on a heap of straw, with his eyes fixed on a beautiful planet, 'which shone like another moon,' and prevailed on him to come in." He complied ;

and immediately on entering the house wrote down, as they now stand, the stanzas " To Mary in Heaven."

Mary Campbell was a poor peasant-girl, whose life had been spent in servile offices, who could just spell a verse in her Bible, and could not write at all,—who walked barefoot to that meeting on the banks of the Ayr, which her lover has recorded. But Mary Campbell will live to memory, while the music and the language of her country endure. Helen of Greece and the Carthage Queen are not more surely immortalized than this plebeian girl.—The scene of parting love, on the banks of the Ayr, that spot where " the golden hours, on angel-wings," hovered over Burns and his Mary, is classic ground ; Vaucluse and Penhurst are not more lastingly consecrated ; and like the copy of Virgil, in which Petrarch noted down the death of Laura, which may have been a pilgrimage but to look on, even such a relic shall be the Bible of Highland Mary. Some far-famed collection shall be proud to possess it ; and many hereafter shall gaze, with glistening eyes, on the handwriting of him,—who by the mere power of truth and passion, shall live in all hearts to the end of time.

HIGHLAND MARY IN FACT AND FICTION.

By DR. WILLIAM FINDLAY.

THE period at which Burns is understood to have made the acquaintance of Mary Campbell was just after his rupture with the Armour family. It is in the knowledge of the whole country-side that Jean is his affianced lover—is, moreover, about to become a mother through him—and holds in her possession a certificate of irregular marriage, which her indignant father, wisely or unwisely, compels her to destroy. Such a crisis, the majority of people would say, was surely a most unbecoming one—to be off with the old love and so enthusiastically on with the new. Neither of the contracting parties in such circumstances, our common-sense tells us, could be very scrupulous, or endowed with the nicest discernment of the fitness of things. Strip the entire episode of the bit of romance with which it is glamoured, and which, I think, is chiefly responsible for leading so many people astray—strip it of the tender and pathetic parting of the lovers by the banks of the Ayr that summer Sunday, on which they exchanged Bibles and plighted everlasting constancy to each other over running, but ominously un-stable, water, and our best-informed ideas of propriety revolt at it. This feeling of revulsion in ourselves is the best explanation of the conduct of Burns. He had no cause to be proud of the affair, but in cooler and more reflective moments, every reason to be ashamed of it. Not that Burns is any greater a sinner in this respect than ourselves, the only difference being that his declensions are known ;

for who is there, I would ask, among us, but would shrink
from having all the love affairs of his "daft young days"
put down in naked black and white for the delectation and
criticism of his enemies. And what applies to Burns affects
with equal force Mary Campbell, who either possessed so
little character or was so weak and infatuated that she took
up with what, to all intents and purposes, was already as
good as a married man, and went through her part of
romantic oath-taking by the banks of the Ayr before going
home to Argyllshire to get ready to marry him—for we
must hold by this accepted version of her home-going until
it has been proved to be incorrect—I say the feeling that
dictated to Burns the observance of a discreet silence applied
with equal force to Mary ; for, be it remembered, all this
dramatic love-making and parting was going on while Jean
Armour was slowly breaking her heart in enforced retire-
ment, and which Mary Campbell, along with the whole
countryside, must have known perfectly well, making it
abundantly evident why a proud-spirited maiden should
wish, like Burns, to preserve a reticence on the entire
subject, although she may not have been strong enough to
abjure it altogether, and tell Burns that she could have
none of him : that his only true and highest duty was to go
and make his peace, for better or for worse, with the dis-
honoured Jean Armour.

The above is the Highland Mary of sober, historical fact,
and commonsense generalisation from said fact. But it is
not the Highland Mary which the Burns-public have been
worshipping for the last hundred years, and toasting at their
Burns Anniversary Festivals. If my readers will only turn
to the first volume of "Ross's Burnsiana," 1892 (Alex.
Gardner, Paisley) which is a general gather-up of floating

Burns literature here and in America, and which contains
verses and essays on, and allusions innumerable to, Highland
Mary, all pitched in the same high admiration key, making
her out everything that was noble, and beautiful, and pure,
and modest ; and gifting to Burns, by virtue of her rare
personality, his best and highest inspiration, and Heaven
only knows what else, he will see what a wrong-headed,
badly-informed class of people the Burns public are who
annually spout all this ideal nonsense about a girl who was,
after all, apparently made of just the ordinary human
"marl" that nine out of every ten of her sisters in and
around Mauchline were.

The Highland Mary of sober, historical fact, is exploded
I should say for ever as a divinity ; and it is the height of
childishness, either to bemoan the catastrophe, or, in our
berobbed feeling, to cast the blame upon those who, by a
plain sifting of facts, have deposed her from a place which
she only occupied through our ignorance. All this, however, unfortunate as we may consider it, has nothing to do
with the fate of the Highland Mary in Burns's songs. She
is immortal, and no forthcoming chain of evidence, be it ever
so complete, or so stained with the frailties of our poor
human nature, can ever touch her. These two personages,
the Mary of fact and the Mary of poetic fiction, must be
kept entirely separate, just because they are two different
personages ; and any revelations, present or future, as to the
character of her of real life cannot affect or destroy our
appreciation of, or enjoyment in, her of poesy. It is on
this very point that the public have so lamentably fallen
into error in persisting in looking upon the two as synony-
mous. I don't deny that Burns himself, the exceptional
conditions of publicity under which he wrote, together with

the fact that there were living models among his neighbours
and acquaintances who, after a fashion at least, stood for
his masterpieces in poem and song, have helped to foster the
belief. And, perhaps, four at least of the five songs (for we
may leave out "Afton Water") bearing on the Mary question—as "A Highland Lassie," "Will ye go to the Indies,
my Mary," "Highland Mary," and "To Mary in Heaven,"
—are responsible for a good deal of direct, personal, and
biographical colour usually associated with the subject of
them. Burns himself admits as much to Thomson—that in
these productions it was not so much the lyric artist that
was speaking as the personal lover. All the same, this
bracketing of the real with the ideal in the public mind
arises because we happen to know. We are in Burns's
secret, so to speak, more deeply than we happen to be in
the case of most other poets—hence these tears. The Mary
of poesy is the poet's impression of her, which (for anything
we know or require to care, indeed, it is not of the slightest
consequence) might bear as little resemblance to her of
fact—the real Mary—as a landscape by Turner might bear
to the real one he painted it from. The poet is not a mere
delineator of what he sees, but an impressionist—if you will,
a creator ; he makes it, in short, hence the complaint of the
common-place that it is not a likeness. If the artist puts
that "light which never was on sea or land" into his
picture, what can the ordinary land-lubber do but condemn
the performance as a likeness of the prosaic land his eye
only knows ? The whole magic lies in the poet's own being.
He takes a Mary, a Jean, a Nanny—or what name you
choose—and in singing their charms and his own passions
to these divinities, he is giving expression to our passions
and painting in rainbow colours our own sweethearts to us,

whom we ourselves have deified in our own imaginations by the power of love, which makes us poets too for the time being.

We often talk, Highland Mary idolators in particular, as if the whole power lay in the object whose beauty, and all the rest of it, simply spoke, automatically almost, through the poet ; whereas it is the poet who sees in the object what nobody else can see—he creates it, makes it, puts it there. In the alchemy of his brain he transmutes everything into gold—a plain-faced rustic maiden into a goddess, just as the genius, the individualism of the artist, by the magic of grouping, arrangement of light and shade, harmonious colouring, leaving this out and putting something else in which has no existence outside his own mind, produces a beautiful work from a piece of common-place landscape which is not really beautiful, but positively ugly as a fact in nature.

This is what Burns did as a lyric artist with his Marys, his Jeans, and his Nannies ; and it is a matter of very little consequence to us, and still less to succeeding generations, whether these earthly originals bore any resemblance or not to the artistic perfections which were created from them or were inspired by them.

SONNET—HIGHLAND MARY.

By JOHN MACFARLANE (John Arbory).

THE brows of Helen from the towers of Troy,
  Shine down the ages like a midnight star,
And veiled in splendours of supernal joy,
  The holy face of Beatrice gleams afar ;
Petrarca's Laura draws us by the might
  Of charm ineffable ; while sweet and strong,
We quaff rich vintages from eyes still bright,
  " Embalmed in amber " of undying song :

But fairer, sweeter by " the gurgling Ayr,"
  One tender form of womanly delight,
Lives by the might of verse forever fair,
  And fresh as ever fell the morning light :
Nor Time nor Death hath aught of conquest here,
  Beneath the heaven of Love's immortal sphere !

THE MONUMENT TO HIGHLAND MARY.

An account of the ceremony connected with the laying of the Foundation Stone.

TUESDAY the Twenty-fifth day of January 1842 witnessed the laying of the foundation stone of the monument to Highland Mary in the old West Churchyard at Greenock. In order to give all possible *eclat* to this ceremonial, invitations had been sent to Masonic bodies in various parts of the country ; and the enthusiasm with which Scotsmen everywhere enter into all matters connected with the memory of their National Poet, brought not a few "brethren of the mystic tie," to the town, to join the local lodges on the great occasion. The Odd-Fellows and Foresters also turned out in considerable numbers, and their appearance, together with the Masons was very imposing. Indeed, the procession consisted almost entirely of the Orders above named, very few of the general public being other than spectators.

In conformity with a previous arrangement, the Committee for the Monument and their friends met in the White Hart Inn, and the Societies and Masonic Lodges in their respective halls, (the Provincial Grand Lodge in the Assembly Rooms, where the preliminary mystic rites were gone through), from whence they proceeded to St. Andrew's Square, where they were marshalled by Captain Mann, Superintendent of Police, in the following order :—

Captain Mann, Marshal.
Town Officers.
Committee of the Monument and the Stewards and other
Admirers of Burns.
Band of Music.

The Independent Order of Odd-Fellows, M.U., as follows :—
Two Heralds on Horseback.
Guardians with Drawn Swords.
St. Andrew's Instrumental Band.
Wardens with Axes.
District Banner.
Past and Present District Officers.
(Regalia carried by Past and Present Officers).
Supporters.   Past Guards.   Supporters.
Supporters.   Noble Guards.   Supporters.
Supporters.   Vice Guards.   Supporters.
Past and Present Secretaries and Assistants.
The Lodge's small Banner.
Brothers Two and Two, with dark clothes, aprons and white
gloves, fingers interlocked.
Finniston Instrumental Band,
Placed Two-thirds distant from the first Band.
Two small District Banners.
Dispensations
Carried by newly initiated Brothers.
Brothers, Two and Two.
Brothers wearing sashes, placed at equal distances along
the line.
Stephen Cooper, C.S., Conductor.

Sub-Conductors.—Brothers Daniel M'Kellar, R. S. Chorley, T. Smith Marshall, Andrew Inglis, William Brown, John Finlay, Robert Moore, Patrick Mooney, Patrick Lyon, David Beggam, James M'Dougall, Robert Gallacher, John Chalmers, Alex. Imrie, James Horn, Hugh Rose, Daniel Sharp, Peter M'Kellar, Samuel Thomson, and John Sim.

———

The Ancient Order of Foresters as follows :—

Three Heralds.

P.C.R. supported by Two Brothers
on Horseback.

S.C.R. supported by two children on Horseback.

Three Beadles with Clubs and Skin Coats.

S.C.R. of 1275, supported by Two Bowmen on foot.

Dispensation,
Supported by Two Brothers.

P. Secretary supported by Two Bowmen.

Two Archers on Horseback.

Band of Music.

Secretary, supported by Two Bowmen.

Emblem, supported by Two Brothers.

Thirty Brothers, Two by Two.

Two Brothers on Horseback.

Emblem, supported by two Bowmen.

Fifty Brothers, Two and Two.

Two Horsemen.

———

Lodges of Freemasons, with their Bands of Music, as
follows :—

Lodges.	R. W. Masters.
Dunoon Argyll,	335, Grigor Harkness, Esq.
Rothesay St. John's,	292, James Smith, Esq.
Dalry Blair,	290, W. F. Blair, Esq.
Star Glasgow,	219, J. C. Russell, Esq.
Airdrie Operative,	203, Matthew Millar, Esq.
Glasgow St. Patrick,	178, Hugh Fleck, Esq.
Greenock St. John,	175, William Johnston, Esq.
Largs St. John,	163, John M'Kirdy, Esq.
Stevenston Thistle and Rose,	169, William Millar, Esq.
Ayr Royal Arch,	163, Andrew Burns, Esq.
Kilbarchan St. Barchan's,	156, Hugh Ferrier, Esq.
Pollokshaws Royal Arch,	153, R. Goagan, Esq.
Glasgow Thistle,	82, James Brown, Esq.
Glasgow St. Mungo,	27, James Alexander, Esq.
Dumbarton,	18, P. H. Mitchell, Esq.

The Provincial Grand Lodge
consisting of
Patrick Maxwell Stewart, Esq., M.P.,
The Most Worshipful Grand Provincial Master.
Robert Wallace, Esq. of Kelly, M.P., Grand Substitute.
Robert Ewing, Esq., Grand P. Past.
Robert Steele, Esq., Grand P. Depute.
The Rev. William Menzies, Grand Chaplain.
David Crawford, Esq., Grand Senior Warden.
Wm. Leitch, Esq., *per* D. M'Dougall, Esq.,
Grand Junior Warden.
Alex. Rodger, Esq., G. P. Treasurer.
John Scott Russell, Esq., Acting Grand Secretary.
Lieut. Hill, R.N., Acting Grand Clerk.

John Campbell, Esq., William Johnstone, Esq., John Black,
Esq., and Donald MacNicoll, Esq., the Grand Masters'
Principal Grand Stewards.
Stewards.—Archibald M. Burrell, Esq., Andrew M. Hunter,
Esq., James M. Scott, Esq., Robert Jamieson, Esq.,
John M'Naughton, Esq., Capt. Campbell, with the
other office-bearers.

The procession left the place of muster in the above order
and proceeded along Rue End, Cathcart, Hamilton, and
West Blackhall Streets—down Ker Street, along Clarence
Street, and down Nicholson Street to the Church-yard. On
arriving at the grave, the Masonic bodies opened up to
allow the Grand Lodge to proceed up the centre to the platform erected near the grave, followed by the Masters and
Wardens of each Lodge, to lay the stone. The Committee
of the Monument first proceeded to the right side of the
stone, supported by the Odd-Fellows and Foresters, whose
gorgeous trappings and lacquered helmets, etc., etc., contributed greatly to the pageant of the day; next followed the
Grand Provincial Lodge, who proceeded to the platform on
the left of the stone; on reaching which, silence being proclaimed, the Grand Chaplain offered up a most beautiful and
appropriate prayer to the Great Architect of the Universe;
after which the splendid band of the 10th Regiment, which
accompanied the Grand Master's Mother Lodge, "The
Greenock St. John's," during the day, played the "Old
Hundred" in the most admirable style. The Acting Grand
Secretary then read a copy of the Inscription, which, along
with a variety of coins and newspapers, were placed in a
bottle hermetically sealed, which the Grand Treasurer deposited in a cavity of the stone. The Grand Master then

walked down from the platform to the east (supported by
his substitute), the Wardens and other office-bearers to the
south and west corners of the stone, with the different im-
plements of the craft, when the stone was lowered into its
bed, and the ceremony of laying was completed by the Grand
Master in the most dignified and impressive manner, accom-
panying the three mystic blows of the mallet with a Masonic
benediction ; after which the Grand Master completed the
whole ceremony by strewing the surface of the stone with
corn and pouring thereon wine and oil, likewise following
the whole with a benediction. The following is the inscription enclosed in the bottle :—

THE STRUCTURE

WHICH IS OVER THIS STONE

HAS BEEN ERECTED

BY THE CONTRIBUTIONS OF MANY ADMIRERS OF

SCOTIA'S BARD,

IN MEMORY OF HIS EARLY LOVE,

MARY CAMPBELL, OR "HIGHLAND MARY."

———

THE FOUNDATION STONE WAS LAID ON THIS

25TH DAY OF JANUARY, 1842,

(BEING THE ANNIVERSARY OF BURNS'S BIRTH)

BY

PATRICK MAXWELL STEWART, ESQ.,

M.P. for Renfrewshire,

AIDED BY THE FOLLOWING COMMITTEE :—

JOHN WHARTON, Collector of Excise in Greenock.

ROBERT WEIR, Stationer in Glasgow.

JOHN INNES and ANDREW PITCAIRN, of Her Majesty's Customs in
Greenock.

ARCHIBALD PATON, of the Excise in Greenock.

ARCHIBALD M'IVER, Bookseller in Greenock.

JOHN MACCUNN, Merchant in Greenock.

JAMES PAGAN, of the *Glasgow Herald* Newspaper in Glasgow.
THOMAS DUNN, Stationer in Glasgow.
WILLIAM MOSSMAN, Sculptor of the Monument.

The ceremony being completed, the Grand Master, with
the other Office-bearers again ascended the platform, the
band at the time playing the Masons' Anthem, after which
Mr. Stewart spoke as follows :—As Provincial Grand
Master, it becomes my duty to address to you a few words
—and they shall be very few—for judging of you by myself,
I am certain that any observations must prove a hindrance
to that flow of memory, and of heartfelt feeling, which this
scene and ceremony are so much calculated to inspire. My
first acknowledgements are due to the gentlemen of the
Committee who suggested this monument, and to whom we
are indebted for its now approaching completion. They
have great merit; Greenock owes them much—Scotland
owes them more; and their best reward will be in the
success of their tasteful and patriotic undertaking. I thank
you all, brethren of all orders and denominations, for your
zealous and able assistance on this occasion. Many of you
have journeyed far to do homage to the memory of " Highland Mary," and none of you, I believe, will grudge having
done so much towards the success of this day's outward
ceremony—for, peculiarly interesting we must all confess it
to be ! The memory of the young, the beautiful, the pious
—Mary Campbell, is inseparably linked with that of our
immortal Poet—Robert Burns ; and it is the irresistible
power of the combined attractiveness of their memories,
that has brought you from your homes and fire-sides, to
assist in distinguishing this grave—where

> Lies mouldering now in silent dust,
> That heart which lo'ed him dearly.

For half a century this spot has remained neglected, although " Highland Mary " has been admired, and loved by every one, of which you are here the witnesses ; and thus has her memory been preserved, and her character transmitted to us by the simple medium of one of those " legends of the heart," which, Burns said, he never polished for fear of defacing. Some, unthinkingly, wondered that we concerted to lay this stone with Masonic honours. For my part I felt that the occasion was peculiarly entitled to our regard. I have ever understood our fraternity to be "a peaceable association, formed for the exercise of mutual benevolence ; and for the purpose of patronizing and executing those structures which have contributed to the amusement or admiration of succeeding ages "—and, if so, what more becoming occasion on which to assemble with one mind, and one heart, could there be than the present ? If the ceremony of laying the foundation stones of colleges and custom-houses and bridges is entitled to Masonic Observance, that of founding monuments to departed genius or virtue is not less so ; and while we have the memory of our great townsman, James Watt, enshrined among us, we cannot forego the humbler work of expressing our delight and proper pride, in holding within our circle the mortal remains of Burns's " Highland Mary." Thus I feel, that as lovers of beauty and purity, of poetry and nature, we are here worthily employed ; and as we journey onwards, the remembrance of this day's ceremony must ever be a welcome inmate in our pensive bosoms. Again, I thank you, brethren of all denominations, for your assistance ; and to the gentlemen of the Committee, I repeat that we are mainly indebted for this national and interesting undertaking, which must prove equally a most attractive ornament of our town and a trophy in the country of Robert Burns.

According to the published programme, the Chairman of the Committee should have returned thanks, but this duty was performed by Mr. Wallace, M.P., who proposed thanks to the Provincial Grand Master for his attendance on the occasion, and for his very eloquent address. He concluded by proposing three cheers to the Committee. His address was much applauded, and at the conclusion the Queen's Anthem was played by the military band. The procession was then reformed in its previous order, and, leaving the Churchyard, proceeded along Ropework and Dalrymple Streets, up William Street to Cathcart Square, where after cheering, the various bodies, with the exception of the Mason Lodges, dispersed. The latter accompanied the Grand Lodge to the Assembly Rooms, at the approach to which they opened up as before, and the Grand Lodge walked up the centre. In the evening a large party dined together in the Coffee-Room, Cathcart Square. P. M. Stewart, Esq., M.P., in the Chair, and Robert Weir, Esq., Glasgow, and John Wharton, Esq., Greenock, Croupiers. The Grand Lodge met in the Assembly Rooms between eight and nine o'clock, presided over by the Provincial Grand Master. The Odd-Fellows supped in the Buck's Head Hall, with Mr. Wallace, M.P., in the Chair, and the Foresters met in the evening in the Gardener's Arms. During the evening the streets continued crowded, bands of music paraded about and the boys amused themselves with discharging fire-works.

PROFESSOR BLACKIE'S TRIBUTE.

. . . . So much for Bonnie Jean.

CONTEMPORARY with this affair, and so closely interwoven
with it that it has been called "an episode," is the romantic
and tragic story of the poet's love for " Highland Mary."
The most natural, as well as the most charitable, way of
interpreting the interlineation of these two loves, is to
suppose with Chambers, that while his heart was bleeding
sorely from what appeared to him the ungenerous and un-
grateful disownment of their connubial bond by bonnie Jean
one of his old flames—for their name was legion—who had
formerly fluttered about him in an easy way, now came to
the front, with the healing power, so strong in woman, and
poured the balm of tender sympathy into his wounds. It is
difficult for any man, especially a man like Burns, to resist
the thrill that passes through him at the touch of a loving
hand on such an occasion.

Mary Campbell, a Highland girl, from the neighbourhood
of Dunoon on the Clyde, "a most sprightly, blue-eyed
creature, of great modesty and self-respect," had been in the
service of his friend, Gavin Hamilton, and was still in the
neighbourhood of Mauchline when that unfortunate affair
with Jean was setting the village in a blaze ; and in adminis-
tering comfort to the widowed heart of the Robert who had
lost his Jean, she presented him as a more than worthy
surrogate for the loss, with Mary, her beautiful self ; and
this Mary had so much faith in the unfortunate young
farmer that she agreed to plight herself to him for life, and

follow him to the Indies, or whithersoever his broken
fortunes might lead him.   It was agreed between them that
she should give up her place, go to the Highlands, where
her father was a sailor in Campbeltown, and arrange matters
there for her formal union with the poet.   The poetical
union had already been completed in a most sentimental and
pious fashion.   On the banks of the Ayr, or in the adjoining
valley of the Faile, the lovers had a meeting on the second
Sunday in May, 1786, where they made the most solemn
vows of faithful adherence.   Standing on each side of a
slow-running brooklet, and holding a Bible between them
the two swore themselves to be one till death.   Mary presented her lover with a plain small Bible in one volume,
while Burns responded with a more dainty one in two
volumes.   The day of this solemn act of devout self-dedica-
tion was the last time that Burns saw his Highland Mary.
No wonder that it remained in his soul for life a picture of
pure affection, more sacred than any with which his large
experience of female favours had furnished him.   Mary
Campbell, after visiting her parents, was returning to
Glasgow, when, stopping on the road at Greenock to attend
a sick brother, she caught fever from him and died.   This
was early in the month of October of the same year in which
her faith was plighted to the poet.   She was buried in the
West Kirkyard of the town, a spot where all who love the
Scottish Muse never fail to drop their fervent tear.

BURNS'S " HIGHLAND MARY."

By J. CUTHBERT HADDEN.

MR. ANDREW LANG has told us that the wives of literary
men and men of genius—the terms are not necessary conver-
tible—are unhappy because their husbands do their work at
home. This admitted cause of domestic disquietude does
not seem to have disturbed so much the serenity of Jean
Armour as the fact that her husband was just a little too
fond of wandering from his own fireside, and that on a
certain date as the years went on he gave himself up to dis-
consolate reminiscences of a departed love, and wrote
rapturous odes to her memory. Even the best of wives
might be pardoned for a slight exhibition of temper when
asked to listen to the rehearsal of an old rival's superior
qualities and virtues ; and Mrs. Burns would have been less
of the woman and more of the angel if she had not, in her
heart at least, resented the terms of those burning strains
addressed to the shade of " Highland Mary " one starry
night in the year of grace 1789. And it was not as if the
poet had been sparing in his female fancies. He has told us
himself that most of his love songs were " the breathings of
ardent passion," and, further, that whenever he wished to
compose a genuine love lyric, which was pretty often, his
source of inspiration lay in the admiration of some beautiful
woman. That was a dangerous kind of inspiration, truly, as
Burns knew to his cost. A poet without a breast full of love

would, of course, be as much of an anomaly as a bird without
wings ; but a poet who falls in love every other day, either
because " he can't help it," or because he desires to draw inspiration from the real, rather than from the ideal, is in
imminent risk of having his heart " vitrified," as Burns
himself puts it.   We are, however, not likely to quarrel
with Burns because he found love-making a necessity of
his life.   It cannot have added much to the happiness of
his wife, but it has done a great deal for the happiness of
the world through the gems of song which were its out-
come.   Take away his love songs and Burns's poetical
legacy to his countrymen would be poor indeed.

The story of Burns's connection with Mary Campbell, the
" Highland Mary " of poetic fame, has in it something of
tragedy as well as romance.   Her unfortunate fate and her
premature death, together with the fact that Burns has made
her the subject of some of his most impassioned verses, have
thrown around her name a halo which only brings into
stronger contrast the obscurity of her early life.   Next to
nothing is known of her career before her meeting with the
poet.   It seems, however, to have been ascertained beyond
doubt that she was born in Dunoon in 1768, her father being
then a seaman on board a revenue cruiser.   The family
ultimately removed to Campbeltown, and there Mary resided
until her seventeenth year, when she went out to service in
the household where Burns made her acquaintance.

Montgomery Castle, known also as Coilsfield, was in the
immediate vicinity of Tarbolton, in the county of Ayr, and,
of course, Mary being a good Christian, attended the parish
kirk with the family on Sundays.   Burns was at this time
working on a farm about midway between Mauchline and
Tarbolton ; and so it happened that, being at church at Tar-

bolton one Sunday, he saw the "interesting young stranger," and was so charmed with her appearance that he determined to make her acquaintance. It has quite recently been remarked how in those days a pining swain might have an opportunity of unburdening his overweighted feelings towards the object of his regard by the aid of a "blackfoot" —a kind of official who could in many cases promote a friend's interest and attend to his own at the same time. In the course of a visit to his own sweetheart a "blackfoot" could secure her influence with a female fellow-servant to consent to a meeting with a companion of his who was sighing for an interview.

It was in this way that Burns secured an introduction to Mary Campbell—an introduction which he seems to have speedily made the most of by the aid of his fascinating eyes and his impassioned eloquence. The intimacy ripened into one of the tenderest kind, and when that famous parting day which has been so often dwelt upon arrived it was as affianced lovers that the pair met and said their farewells. The story has frequently been told how, on the second Sunday of May, 1786, the poet and his Mary were found together in a picturesque spot on the banks of a little stream near "the castle of Montgomery," spending what proved to be their last hours together. They stood one on either side of the water, laved their hands in the current, and holding a Bible between them, vowed everlasting fidelity. It is to this meeting that Burns refers in the well-known lines :

> That sacred hour can I forget ?
> Can I forget the hallowed grove,
> Where by the winding Ayr we met,
> To live one day of parting love ?

> Eternity will not efface
> Those records dear of transports past ;
> Thy image at our last embrace —
> Ah ! little thought we 'twas our last !

On that final parting day the lovers presented each other with a Bible, appropriately inscribed ; and the poet's gift, after having made two journeys across the Atlantic and experiencing a very singular career, is now preserved in the monument at Ayr. On the flyleaf are two texts of Scripture—" Ye shall not swear by My name falsely, I am the Lord," and " Thou shalt not forswear thyself, but shalt perform unto the Lord thine oaths." The writing owing in part no doubt to continued exposure to the light, has almost faded out of sight, and probably in a few years more it will have vanished entirely. This would be a great misfortune, and we see no reason why the visitors to the monument should not be satisfied with a look of the volume without seeing the all but imperceptible autograph. What has become of Mary's gift to Burns no one seems to know : not even that little relic has survived her romantic career.

In the autumn following the meeting of the lovers near Montgomery Mary Campbell went home to Campbeltown to make some preparations for her union with the poet. In the October of the same year (1786) she went to Greenock, accompanied by her father, was immediately laid down with fever, and died before the poet could be summoned to her side. She is said to have been quite sensible during her last hours, and just before the end came she said to her cousin : " If it had been God's will I would have liked to be Robert Burns's wife ; but I know I am dying, and I am quite willing." Mary was laid to rest in the West Churchyard of

Greenock, which has thus become one of the shrines at which the admirers of Burns love to pay their devotions. In 1842 a monument was erected over the grave, representing the parting of the lovers at Montgomery, and bearing the words :

> Oh ! Mary, dear departed shade !
> Where is thy place of blissful rest ?

More recently the local Burns Club had the grave dressed and planted with flowers, but the ground having sunk below the surrounding level was unfavourable to successful growth and the hollow has now been filled up with white boulders resting on a base of cement. An exceedingly beautiful statuette of the poet and his Mary was executed by Mr. Hamilton MacCarthy of Toronto, for the late Senator John MacDonald, and a life-size reproduction in marble of the same design has just been finished for Mr. Walter M'Farlane, of Glasgow.

THE BANKS OF AYR AND HIGHLAND MARY.

Of all the soul-stirring lyrics which Scotland's chief minstrel has written, those of the pure-minded Highland lassie excel all others by an immense distance. We have heard them sung in infancy, and love to hear them in our old age. They, when put together, form a tale of pity so melting that we may safely say the man whose heart is not touched, his passions not softened, and a loftier view of human nature not taken, is lost to the ennobling influence of poetry and song. And if he is to any extent an admirer of Robert Burns, he will feel that the poet has left us a heritage of goodness that redeems him from much of that frailty that he wept over himself, and which we sorrowfully lament.

In writing of the song scenery of our native land we are attracted to the scenery of which so much has been written so feelingly. The banks of the Ayr round about the Castle of Montgomery are pretty—it would be well to say lovely— and we wend our way, to us, the dearest spot on its banks. Yet it is not the earliest tourist district to reach. There are as yet no special trains to carry their thousands of noisy occupants to the sacred resort where the bard and Mary met to spend one parting day and dedicate themselves to each other for life. Let us go by ourselves, Sandy and I. The day is beautiful ; we had parted with the minister of Mauchline, and were just in that fine flow of spirits which arises from contact with the good and kindly. The road improves as we journey on. The ingathering of the crops is cheerily going on. Before us a smart lass is driving home a well-laden cart of corn. "Ah," says Sandy, "that's one of Burns's Ayrshire lasses ; we will make up to her and hae a chat just to see if the memory of Rabbie still lives among the young anes of the country." We do make up to her, and it is needless to say get a surprise. Like well-bred men as we pretend to be, one glance, and we pass to the usual salutations of the day. We tell her where we are going, and our object in going to Coilsfield. She was a blythe woman and a hearty one ; entered into our projects heartily ; chatted away so freely that before we parted we felt quite at ease in letting her know we were disappointed in not find-ing her a young lass. I wish some of the Clydebank bachelors had heard her hearty laugh, and then her outburst of "I am fifty ; but mind, don't forget to find Heelan' Mary's thorn." Yes, the memory of the bard is still a strength in this part of Ayrshire. Soon we reach the point where the river touches the highway between Mauchline and Ayr, and here it is joined by the little water of Faile. This small stream sweeps past the mansion of Coilsfield, which is rather a Grecian edifice than a baronial castle of the olden time. The bard has taken the poet's license here to a little extent. It lies a short distance from the farm of Mossgiel, and midway between Mauchline and Tarbolton. At Moss-giel it will be seen that Burns was in dangerous proximity to more than one of his enslavers. There is little to rest upon to enable us to form a thoroughly correct view of the poet's relation to the object of such fervid, and, let me say, lasting attachment. Be it what it may, we would not for all he has written otherwise have missed the songs he has written on Mary Campbell. Mary was dairymaid at Coilsfield. After he had been discarded by the Armour family he renewed an acquaintance he had formed with

Mary, and they agreed to be married. She went home to
arrange for the wedding, caught a fever, and died at
Greenock, to the lasting sorrow of Burns. The solem-
nity of the meeting, and the disappointment following
completely upset the poet, and had it not been that, amidst
the gloom of that time, a break took place in the clouds
hovering above and around him, the career of Scotia's most
gifted singer would have been different than it was. He
had already written :

> Will ye go to the Indies, my Mary,
> And leave auld Scotia's shore ;
> Will ye go to the Indies, my Mary,
> Across the Atlantic's roar ?

It is very many years, we were quite boys, when the
story of Burns's Bible (given to Mary at parting) were still
in the hands of Mary's relatives, but they were in Canada,
whither they had been taken long ago. But the far-distant
relative with a zeal and patriotism worthy of the highest
praise, agreed to restore them to Scotland, where the
admirers of the lovers will have looked upon them with
touching interest as they rest in the monument on the banks
of the Doon. Of all the relics of the poet they are the most
precious left to us, containing as they do the evidence
of ardent, fond affection, rent asunder by an inscrutable
providence. There is the little stream, the Faile, and where
it joins the Ayr the scene is one of those pretty ones so often
met with in Scotland. But when burthened with thoughts
of the past—of what is, and what might have been—one
seeks privacy, and even the presence of an intimate is felt
to be an intrusion. Standing on the banks of the river on
the fine autumn day we feel like the poet,

" Here simmer first unfaulds her robes,
And there they longest tarry ;
For there I took my last farewell
Of my sweet Highland Mary."

But let us do more—let us put on record the mind of the
poet himself on this matter. To his publisher he writes :—
" This song is founded on a passage of my youthful days,
and I own that I would be much flattered by seeing the
verses set to an air that would ensure celebrity," true again
to the memory of his Highland Mary. Sitting down by the
banks of the Ayr, rapt in meditation, I see my companion
strolling away by the side of the river musing doubtless, on
the time and last occasion of the lovers' meeting. After a
time we leave the sacred grove and make for the house. A
gentleman, whom we accosted, said—" The gate into Coilsfield is open ; no one will hinder you : just go in." So did
we find, and we entered. No challenge nor interruption,
we pass the front of the house, and make for Tarbolton,
where is the house that formed the "howf" of the poet,
and the Masonic Club he so finely celebrated when he took
his " Farewell of the brethren." This was the hour before
the dawn of his brilliant, though oft-clouded, life. To these
much sorrowing strains, arising from the contemplated
exile, we owe much of his saddening poetry. Saddening
but tender, as we read we feel that this contemplated exile
has shown us the bard in his loftiest strain.

" Farewell auld Scotia's bleak domains,
Far dearer than the torrid plains
Where rich ananas blow.
Farewell a mother's blessing dear,
A brother's sigh, a sister's tear,
My Jean's heart-rending throe !"

As we leave the village of Tarbolton the shades of evening are falling around us, and we are reminded of the
words—

> " Adieu ! a heart-warm fond adieu !
>   Dear brothers of the mystic tie,
> Ye favoured, ye enlightened few,
>   Companions of my social joy.
>
> Though I to foreign lands must hie,
>   Pursuing fortune's sliddery ba',
> With melting heart and brimful eye
>   I'll mind ye still, though far awa'."

When the tourist visits this locality, he will, as we did, find
Tarbolton is not of itself an attractive village, but all round
it is made dear to the admirer of the poet, for he will be
touching on Willie's Mill, and look over to Lochlea; he will
be walking by the farm of Mossgiel, and the neighbours will
be ready to tell him that in the field he is passing the poet
turned up the " Wee Moosie." He will find, in fact, that
Scotia's most gifted bard is still the favourite of the people
whose virtues he has adorned, and of whose failings he himself was an unfortunate illustration. We left the banks of
the Ayr, the Castle o' Montgomery, and many other scenes
with the full determination that our visit would not be the
last to the sacred spot, where, as he says—

> " Ayr, gurgling, kiss'd his pebbly shore
>   O'erhung with wild woods, thick'ning green,
> The fragrant birch and hawthorn hoar
>   Twined amorous 'round the raptured scene."

HIGHLAND MARY.

By JOHN ARNOT.

At a Greenock Burns celebration, Mr. John Arnot, in proposing "The Memory of Highland Mary," said that of the
many towns more or less associated with Burns — Ayr,
Irvine, Mauchline, Kilmarnock, Edinburgh, and Dumfries
—Greenock might take a very high place. Ayr had the un-
speakable honour of having given him birth ; Kilmarnock
issued his first edition ; Edinburgh lionised him, and then
somewhat contemptuously neglected him ; Dumfries sheltered him in his last weary years—there the "respectables"
shunned him while living and afterwards gave him a great
funeral ; and Greenock found "a place of blissful rest" for
the remains of the one woman who really had his heart.
Greenock had a great trust in the Old West Kirkyard, where
near by stood the only church of the pre-Reformation period
in town. In the place where "the rude forefathers of the
hamlet sleep," and within sound of hundreds of hammers
and the roar of machinery, lay the dust of her who had become a great literary fact, to whose shrine thousands of
people gathered from all parts of the world. Various complaints had appeared from time to time in the newspapers
about the neglect of Highland Mary's grave by the Greenock
Burns Club, but these complaints, so far as the Club was
concerned, had no foundation. The kirk-session of the Old
West Kirk was the obstacle that stood in the way. In clos-
ing, Mr. Arnot said :—Mary Campbell's worth, her nobility
of character, her grace of disposition, and her comely form

served to do more for Burns than all the ministers and kirk-sessions of his time—she struck the loftiest chords in his nature, the chords of trust, of devotion, and of that inner religious feeling of which he had really more than some of the fault-finding Pharisees who take care to remember and to recite all his grave errors, while they discreetly conceal their own. " Whatever faults," says a very candid critic, " may attach to Burns, not the slightest speck has ever been found to stain the character of his Highland Mary ; and she stands enshrined in the temple of Romantic Poesy in all the spotless purity of Parian marble." This dictum is only the severe and simple truth. If Mary Campbell did not write poetry she *lived* it. She showed Robert Burns—and, through the medium of his powerful genius, all men—that

> " 'Tis only noble to be good.
> Kind hearts are more than coronets,
> And simple faith than Norman blood."

Our immortal poet knew this, and his love for her was singularly lofty in its ideal, and was, while intensely ardent, as high, as elevated as an Alpine peak, as pure as the snow on its summit.

BURNS AND HIS HIGHLAND MARY.

By G. WASHINGTON MOON.

THE mountain lake, which seems asleep in love,
  And dreaming, murmurs to the pebbly shore
Its tender passion for the clouds above,
  Which stoop to kiss it, and at sunrise soar
  Away to heaven, hears oft the tempest roar,
And rouses till its bound'ries are o'erleapt ;
  But soon is calm and loving as before—
So, too, the poet's soul by passion's breath was swept ;
But calmed itself again, as if in love it slept.

He breathed out war, and whispered love's soft vows ;
  He poured forth satires, and wrote hymns of praise ;
He wailed the dirge, and sang the mad carouse ;
  And told of "palaces," and " banks and braes."
  But " Auld lang syne," and suchlike touching lays,
Reveal the nature whence they all did flow—
  Who has not heard his song of other days,
So quaintly sweet, "John Anderson, my jo ?"
Nor felt, " How true the heart that could have written so ! "

Ay ! true indeed : and loving as 'twas true,
  How bright a picture of his heart we see
In that brief hour wherein he bids adieu
  To her whose lover he was proud to be—

9

Dear " Highland Mary " of fond memory ;
Ere many months they hoped to be united,
　　And dwell together 'neath their own roof-tree.
They met, to part awhile ; and vows were plighted—
They never met again ! Chill death that sweet flow'r blighted.

The twining branches o'er their heads were waving ;
　　They stood beside a purling silv'ry brook ;
And, its waters clear, their clasped hands laving,
　　They held between them God's all-sacred book ;
　　And vowing to be faithful, fondly took
A last embrace ! Ever as she did gain
　　Each distant height, she turned with ling'ring look ;
He, after her, his tearful eyes did strain ;—
And so the lovers parted, ne'er to meet again !

The mem'ry of this scene would ever fill
　　His heart with all the agony of woe.
Honour to Burns ! his name is cherished still.
　　What though he lived a century ago :
　　Time, in its onward and resistless flow,
Only the more the poet's name endears !
　　Honour to Burns !—'tis all we can bestow :—
Sighs for his sorrows ; for his loss, our tears ;
Praise, for his deathless songs ; and, for his memory, cheers.

BURNS' HIGHLAND MARY.

FROM "RAMBLES IN EUROPE."

By LEONARD A. MORRISON.

GREENOCK is naturally interesting. But not its native beauty alone would cause the traveller to prolong his stay. That which gives it its celebrity is the fact that in its old cemetery lies buried one, attractive in herself, whom the love and adoration of one man, with the magic of his pen, have made immortal, whose resting-place is historic, and to which pilgrims come from every clime. It is the grave of Mary Campbell, the dairy-maid, known to the world over as Burns's " Highland Mary," one who was to have been his bride. He loved his Highland Mary with a constancy which never faltered in its devotion, which from its nature could know no death. When her footsteps faltered, when her feet touched the cold waters of the river of death, then he " trod the wine-press " of sorrow alone, and from his suffering soul came forth the purest, truest sentiments he ever expressed. The dross was burned away, the pure gold was revealed, the diamond shone with brightest lustre. On the anniversary of the day on which he heard of her death he gave expression to his feelings in an address to " Mary in Heaven."

In " David Copperfield " Steerforth said, " Think of me at my best," a custom not always followed " in the corrupted currents of this world." This poem showed Burns at his

best. From this deep grief, his great loss, and abiding
sorrow, his anguished spirit found expression in one of the
sweetest laments ever penned. The pathos of no sweeter
song ever made responsive chords in human hearts vibrate
with livelier sympathy. For him life's grief, life's loss, life's
great calamity, brought their compensation ; they developed
and revealed in him a sympathy, tenderness, and nobility
never dreamed of before. Had Mary lived, that poem would
never have been written. That evidence of the deep tenderness of his nature, that monument of his genius, would
not excite the sympathy and admiration of all time. As
a consequence the world forgives much in the life and
character of Burns.

In the Old West Kirk cemetery is her grave. Above her
rises a marble shaft, with figures representing her last parting from Burns, and below is a poetical quotation.

ERECTED

OVER THE GRAVE OF

HIGHLAND MARY,

1842.

" My Mary, dear departed shade,
Where is thy place of blissful rest ? "

An iron railing surrounds the lot. With the permission of
the guide I cut a few leaves from the shrub which grew
above her, and pressing them out carefully I sent them to
widely separated friends in the United States as precious
momentoes of her, the loved of Burns, who was cut down in
her beautiful youth ?

The kirk is an ancient structure, founded in 1589. James
Watt, the utilizer of steam, is there buried. Among the

surnames on tombstones familiar to us in America are those of Peter Campbell, John Brown, John Morrison, Malcolm M'Gregor, James Ramsay, and John Allison. Members of the Jamieson family and others, are among the quiet sleepers.

ON SEEING A LOCK OF HIGHLAND MARY'S HAIR.

By ANNA M. SMITH.

OH, thou fair lock, thou tress of palish gold !
  What thronging memories come at sight of thee !
How is the scroll of Time again unrolled,
  Revealing that which never more can be !

I see thee waving round a brow of snow,
  As gently by the summer wind caressed,
And wanton o'er a cheek of softest glow,
  Or nestle loving on a poet's breast.

And once again the hawthorn's snowy bough
  Scatters its sweets upon the summer air ;
Again I hear the poet's raptured vow
  That bids thee know that "bliss beyond compare."

And thou hast felt the throb of that great heart,
  That Sorrow's darkest frown could not subdue,
But braving angry Fortune's fiercest dart,
  Was still to manhood and affection true.

Oh, Scotia ! well mayest thou love thy rustic bard ;
  For who, like he, has told it far and wide,
What generous bosoms, noble hearts and true,
  Are wont beneath the hodden-grey to hide ?

How thine own children, in their lowly shades,
  At Poverty's chill fount may oft have drank,
But "blessed with health and peace and sweet content,"
  May still defy the guinea-stamp of rank.

Oh, wond'rous bard ! thy genius—spark divine—
  Does still this very atmosphere pervade ;
And its light thy human frailties tine
  As morn's obscuring mists before the sun must fade.

Oh, Scotia ! as in the years Time's ceaseless course has run,
  Through what may come to thee by Fortune's turns,
Acknowledge him thy own, thy darling son,
  And still adore the name of ROBERT BURNS !

HIGHLAND MARY'S GRAVE.

FROM THE "GREENOCK TELEGRAPH."

THE grave of Highland Mary in the Old West Churchyard,
with the beautiful monument at its head, is perhaps one of
the most attractive spots in Greenock ; and that being the
case, it is somewhat astonishing to find that so little interest
is taken in it by the great bulk of the inhabitants.   It is
one of the few shrines to which the more ardent admirers of
Burns make periodical pilgrimages.   Around it there linger
the most hallowed associations connected with the memory
of our national poet ; and to the lovers of his works that
quiet resting-place—where

> " Mouldering now in silent dust,
>   That heart that lo'ed me dearly,"

—is held in reverence almost as great as her memory was
cherished by the poet when he was alive.   It is visited year
after year by large numbers of people from all parts, includ-
ing Scotchmen who have settled down in America, Australia
and other countries, all anxious to pay tribute at the tomb
of the woman who inspired the poem in which occur the
lines placed on the front of the monument—

> " Oh, Mary ! dear departed shade !
>   Where is thy place of blissful rest ? "

It is one of the few sights with which we in Greenock can
entertain our friends from a distance.   It is no great credit

to us, therefore, that up till this year the piece of ground surrounding the monument has been kept in anything but a tidy condition. Some members of the Gardeners' Society or a few of the more enthusiastic gentlemen of the Greenock Burns Club have from time to time bestowed some little care on the sacred spot; but as there was no regularity in these efforts, they only served to show more distinctly the necessity which existed for something being done to keep the grave permanently in a respectable condition. A number of years ago the members of the Greenock Burns Club, who have all along taken a greater interest in the grave than they got credit for, tried to get liberty to take it under their charge and keep it in order. But there were difficulties in the way at that time. They again made an effort in the same direction this year, and it is satisfactory to know that on this occasion they have been more successful. They have now obtained liberty to keep the grave in proper order; and, what is more, they have set about taking advantage of the privilege which has been granted them, and through one of their members, Mr. G. M. Butler, and at considerable expense, have turned what was to all appearance a waste piece of ground into a tastefully cultivated little plot which it is a decided pleasure to look upon. As is generally known, the monument—which, by the way, was erected by public subscription in 1842—is surrounded by a railing enclosing a small piece of ground, and that ground has now been decorated in the most appropriate manner by flowers and plants loved and sung of by the poet. The rail has been intertwined with Ayrshire roses and honeysuckle, of which Burns sings in "Ye Banks and Braes"—

" To see the rose and woodbine twine ; "

and in his " Epistle to John Lapraik "—

>" While briers and woodbines budding green."

Inside the rail there is a row of that "wee, modest, crimson-tipped flower," the daisy, white and red—

>" Yet all beneath the unrivalled rose,
>, The lowly daisy sweetly blows,"

—and then in the centre a solid green-sward turf, emblematic of the lines—

>" Now green's the sod and cauld's the clay
>That wraps my Highland Mary !"

In the middle of the sod is planted a single-stemmed thorn, bringing to mind another line—

>" How rich the hawthorn's bloom "

—from the same poem—the song which celebrates in such beautiful strains the last meeting of Burns and Mary Campbell on the banks of Ayr, and of which the poet says in a letter to a friend :—" This song pleases me ; I think it is in my happiest manner. The subject of the song is one of the most interesting passages of my youthful days ; and I own I should be much flattered to see the verses set to an air which would ensure celebrity. Perhaps, after all, it is the still growing prejudice of my heart that throws a borrowed lustre over the merits of the composition." This thorn does not obstruct the view, and comes in exceedingly well with the other poetical surroundings. On either side of the small stone below the monument four plants of the rough burr thistle find a place ; and in the autumn, when the tomb is usually visited by a great many strangers, these hardy flowers, so dear to the true Scottish heart, will be in bloom and will look extremely well. Of them Burns wrote :—

> " The rough burr thistle, spreading wide,
> Amang the bearded bear ;
> I turned the weeder clips aside
> And spared the emblem dear."

Then a few primroses, which Burns mentions in "The Posie" and "Afton Water," are planted near the top of the grave, along with several bunches of sweet-smelling thyme, of which the poet sings in "Kellyburn Braes"—

> " Hey, and the rue grows bonnie wi' thyme."

In addition to the flowers and plants with which the grave has already been adorned, a space is left for other flowers to be planted as the summer advances. Even now, however, the improvement which has been effected is very great. The piece of ground around the monument is not so extensive as might have been wished, but it has been set off to the best possible advantage, and along with the two beautiful lime trees, fresh laden with their summer foliage, with which the monument is flanked, looks very nice indeed—presents an appearance, in fact, which will harmonise with the feelings of the admirers of our national bard when they visit the Old West Churchyard to look upon the last resting-place of one who was held in such high esteem by Burns while she lived, whose death he so deeply lamented, and whose memory he cherished as one of his most sacred possessions.

www.ingramcontent.com/pod-product-compliance
Lightning Source LLC
Chambersburg PA
CBHW030601270326
41927CB00007B/1004